Cultural Perception
of
Mental Illness

Cultural Perception

of

Mental Illness

West African Immigrants in Philadelphia Perspective

DR. PATRICK CHINEDU DURU

Library of Congress Control Number: 2020913778

HARDBACK: 978-1-952155-64-2
PAPERBACK: 978-1-952155-63-5
EBOOK: 978-1-952155-65-9

Ordering Information:

For orders and inquiries, please contact:
1-888-404-1388
www.goldtouchpress.com
book.orders@goldtouchpress.com

Printed in the United States of America

TABLE OF CONTENTS

CHAPTER ONE
STATEMENT OF THE PROBLEM

CHAPTER TWO
REVIEW OF RELATED LITERATURES

CHAPTER THREE
METHODOLOGY

CHAPTER FOUR
DATA ANALYSIS

CHAPTER FIVE
RESULTS SUMMARY

CHAPTER SIX
WORK YET TO BE DONE

CHAPTER SEVEN
BIBLIOGRAPHY AND SOURCES

CHAPTER EIGHT
APPENDICES

TABLES AND FIGURES

DEDICATION

This academic research work is dedicated to all men and women who care for the wellbeing of the sick.

ACKNOWLEDGMENT

I thank Almighty God for His graces enabling me to do this researching and writing. I am very grateful to God for the guidance, protection, and care throughout my studies.

I thank my wife Agatha Duru and my children, Evan and Colette, for their steadfast support throughout my studies, researching and writing.

In a particular way, I thank the staff and faculty members of the Graduate Theological Foundation for the enormous knowledge I gained from them. I thank especially my Project Consultant/Supervisor, Prof. Fr. Anthony Nwachukwu Ph.D. Psy.D. for his strict but professional guidance and supervision in writing this academic research paper.

Moreover, I thank Ronke for her encouragements and support in sourcing articles for my research and academic growth.

My appreciation also goes to the Catholic Charismatic group members of St. Barnabas Catholic Church in South West Philadelphia for their prayers and contributions towards my academic success. My thanks also go to the Parish Priests of St. Barnabas Catholic Church Fr. Carlos Benites, Fr. Mariano Dellagiovanna and Fr. Migal Bravo for their prayers and support.

I am grateful to all the participants that were interviewed in writing this academic research paper.

I thank God for my late parents, Mr. Emmanuel Duru and Mrs. Margret Duru, for training me to work hard to achieve success in life.

ABSTRACT

Mental illness is a big issue in West Africa with the perceived notion that demons, witchcraft attack, and curses are responsible for mental illnesses. It is these perceived notions about mental illness that cause stigmatization and stereotypes against persons diagnosed with mental illness and their families. The negative perception of mental illness also causes non-diagnoses and treatment of the disease in West Africa. There is also the belief that mentally ill people are dangerous and can sporadically attack another person, and it is the reason they are unemployed or get proper medical attention. Another negative perception about mental illness in West Africa is that it is untreatable and transferrable to other people; hence, they are socially stigmatized and discriminated from relating to others. Thus, a mentally designated seems to behave true to type.

The study identified the cause of the negative perception of mental illness to lack of mental health facilities, poverty, bad government policy, and harmful cultural notion about mental illness. The most significant cause of mental illness in West Africa is the lack of knowledge of different types and causes of mental illness. However, the study used 18 participants from different countries in West Africa to understand the cultural perception of mental illness in West Africa. It was so extensive that each of these 18 sampled participants equally co-opted 8 other participants for our consideration and analysis, bringing the total number to 144 participants. The result obtained was astonishing. Without pre-empting our chapters three and four at this point, it is necessary to note that after the researcher affected the redistribution and validation of data obtained, our reliability index approximately came to 140 participants, in which higher percentage (87%) of the participants believe that the cause of the mental illness was a demonic attack, witchcraft, or curses. Also, a high percentage (54%) believes that mental illness is untreatable, while the highest percentage (89%) thinks that the stigma against mentally ill persons in West Africa is a problem. The study overall account also shows that 87% of mentally ill people are unacceptable at job places, socially avoided, and denied proper medical treatment.

The result of the study shows that poverty, lack of education, bad government policy on mental illness, and stigma are the major hindrances to mental illness treatment in West Africa. It is also the reason most mentally ill people seek services of traditional healers for treatment. The result also shows that being compassionate to mentally ill people, education, advocacy; good government policy on mental illness, provision of adequate health care, food, shelter, and clothing will decrease mental health issues in West Africa.

GENERAL INTRODUCTION

Mental illness perceptions and stigmatization have been in existence for many years in West Africa (Stefanovic et al., 2016; Achiga, 2016; Gur et al., 2012)). The contrary opinion on mental illness in West Africa originated from their ancestors and had continued to the present generation (Oduguwa, Adedokun & Owigbodun, 2017). The notion of mental illness among West African people is that mental illness is non-treatable, transferable, and a sign of bad omen to the family and society (Kadri et al., 2004). The little notice that a person has mental illness in the family generates internal stigmatization to the individual, the family, friends, and the community (Barke, Nyarko & Klecha (2011) at large.

The first type of stigma against the mentally ill in West Africa is avoidance (Gureje et al., 2005. People from West Africa perceive that those with mental illness are dangerous and can attack another person at any time (Achiga, 2016). The mentally ill types of stigma include – social avoidance, deprivation of needs like clean clothes, housing, and healthful foods. The health care professionals and schools also avoid individuals diagnosed with mental illness in West Africa. The stigma by mental health professionals often leads to unsatisfactory or non-treatment of those with mental illness.

The World Health Organization (WHO) estimated that mental illness is the third leading cause of disease in the world, especially in Africa. The WHO statistics show that about one in 7 children and adolescents in West Africa have difficulties, and 1 in 10 persons experience psychiatric disorder. The Center for Disease Control

(CDC, 2010) reported that African experience the highest level of depression (12.8%) in the world. The rates of mental illness in countries of West Africa correspond to the total number of mental illness in the world as a whole. It is this awareness that calls for urgent need to bring it to notice on the dangers of neglect in terms of diagnosis and treatment of those diagnosed with mental illness in West Africa.

There are negative perceptions and stigmatization against the mentally ill persons by people from West Africa (World Health Organization, 2012). The understanding factor for the contrary opinion on mental illness among immigrants from West Africa is that mental illness is not treatable but associated with curses, demon-possessed or witchcrafts (Stefanovic et al., 2016; Achiga, 2016)). It is the negative perceptions of mental illness that makes the mentally ill persons in West African countries not diagnosed or treated (Stefanovics et al., 2016). The negative perceptions of mental illness in West Africa also lead to stigmatization and other forms of brutality against mentally ill individuals ((Gyanfi, Hegadoren & Park. 2018; Gureje et al., 2005).

The World Health Organization explained that most people with mental illness experience stigma and discrimination (Gyanfi et al., 2018) and it is the third leading cause of illness in the world (WHO, 2012). One of the reasons for the negative perception of mental illness among West Africans is due to inadequate or lack of mental health facilities and professionals to care for the mentally sick individuals in their respective countries (Agyapong et al., 2015). The governments in West Africa have not taken proper notice to understand that mental illness is not a taboo, but treatable disease. It is the ignorance by the government in West Africa that makes them not to invest financially in the diagnosis and treatment of mentally ill persons. The government policy on mental health is also not well defined in most countries in West Africa, and most countries in West Africa do not have a mental health center to refer the mentally sick for counseling, diagnoses, and treatment. In addition to the lack of mental health centers, lack of trained mental health personals or professionals hinders adequate treatment of the mentally ill persons (Walker, 2015).

Consequently, it has become inexpedient to observe that, according to Dr. Alexis Carrel, a Physician, Biologist, and Psychoanalyst, on his advocacy and insistence for human quality reproduction, upraising of correct children, race betterment and fitness, admitted that: "Every normal human being has some percentage of madness" (*Man, the Unknown,* New York: NY: Harper & Bros Press, 1935:319). This strongly noted observation helps us to understand that at the background of human interactions, relationships, and activities, the madness of so many mentally rich people may always be circumvented and misinterpreted as having other psychological temperaments except being addressed as mentally ill. In other words, while poor fellows within needy circumstances can easily be classified as mentally ill ones, the well-placed in society are respectfully not.

The countries in West Africa that have established mental health policy, lack of proper mental health implementation hinder mental illness treatment (Walker, 2015). Also, the problem of reduced salaries and benefits to the few mental health professionals make them travel out of their respective countries to seek better financial reward from other countries; hence the treatment of psychological sickness is hard to attain.

Another problem that causes the non-recognition of mental illness as sickness and improper treatment of mental illness is poverty. The statistics among the countries in West Africa shows that mental illness is most prevalent in rural areas where also the rate of poverty is very high (Eaton et al., 2017). The debt coupled with the negative perception makes the mentally sick not to seek a solution to the cure of mental sickness (Lund et al., 2013).

The negative perceptions on mental sickness by West Africans are rooted in their ancestors' beliefs, and it has continued to be acceptable even among the educated ones (Oduguwa, Adedokun & Owigbodun, 2017). The myth about mental illness often leads to the stigmatization in question against the mentally sick persons and their families through avoidance by relatives, friends, and the society (Gureje et al., 2005; Gyanfi et al., 2018). The stigma associated with mental illness can lead to avoidance from family members of someone diagnosed with mental illness to get married (Kadri et al., 2004). There is a perception that mental illness is inheritable, and marrying from the family of a mentally ill person will make it transferrable to the other family (Kadri et al., 2004).

The significant cause of the negative perception of mental illness is the lack of education (Achiga, 2016). According to the WHO, the lack of schooling possesses the greatest hindrance to mental illness understanding, diagnoses, and treatment (Gyanfi et al., 2018). The combination of lack of knowledge, poverty, and mental health facilities causes the greatest hindrance in mental illness treatment in West Africa (Gyanfi et al., 2018). It is the economic hardship among most families especially those that have a spiritual ill person that makes them go and seek treatment with quacks or traditional healers who do not know about mental illness treatment (Eaton et al., 2017; Agyapong et al., 2015), to the point that young girls with very bright futures have ended up by being married to these well advanced and aged traditional healers as their wives because of mental illness. These conventional healers or native doctors use incantations, herbs, and sometimes flogging to cast out the presumed demons on the mentally sick as a mode of treatment (Asuni, 1990). The traditional healers that use herbs are untrained on the dosage and side effects of what they are prescribing for the sick ones and it may compound the problem (Asuni, 1990).

The negative perception of mental illness by West Africa calls for clinicians and counselors to educate the people on mental health types, causes, diagnosis, and treatment. It will involve helping to dispel the rumors that have been going on among West Africans that mental illness is inheritable, untreatable or associated with a demon. It is with proper education and provision of good mental health centers that the problem of stigmatization will decrease (Kabir et al., 2004; Yendork, Kpobi & Sarfo, 2016). Also, counselors and clinicians should advocate for the less privileged families among the citizen of West Africa that have a mentally ill person as to have subsidized cost in treatment for mental illness. Counselors and clinicians should also advocate that mentally ill persons should be shown 'love' through the provision of good food, housing, and proper treatment.

The most significant cause of the negative perception against mentally ill persons is due to a lack of education (Kabir et al., 2004). In West African countries, inadequate or lack of proper knowledge leads to lack of understanding of mental illness prognosis, types, diagnoses, and treatment of mental illness. It is the lack of education that causes persons with mental illness in West Africa to flock to traditional healers for treatment. The negative perception among West African immigrants residing in the Philadelphia region on mental illness is not different from their counterparts back home that demons, curses, witchcraft attack, and drugs are responsible for mental illness. It is worrisome that even with their education in the western world, immigrants still have a negative perception of mental illness. Some of the negative opinions on mental illness come as a result of religious beliefs on demons. The instance of Jesus casting out demons from a man possessed by an evil spirit (Luke 4:33-37) leads to the influence of religion on mental illness perceptions. In the Bible passage, the mad man used to throw stones to bystanders, and people avoid him. It was on the bases of the Bible account of the mad man throwing stones to people that make people of West Africa avoid the mentally ill as being dangerous. The belief among West African people that demons cause mental illness also makes the mentally ill person go for deliverance and prayers in churches or mosques. Also, the notion that curses or evil spirit attacks cause mental illness makes those diagnosed with mental illness to seek remedy from traditional healers. They believe that the biogenic treatment as used in the western world is not effective in the treatment of mental illness makes the mentally ill to seek remedy from quacks that are unaware of the dosage or side effects of their prescription. The most traumatized problem of mental illness diagnosis in West Africa is that of stigmatization, as could better be explained in the research parameters in chapter one.

CHAPTER ONE

STATEMENT OF THE PROBLEM

The Igbo of Nigeria always says that "*Awo anaghi agba oso ihihe n'efu*", meaning that the toad does not run in broad day time for nothing". That is to say, either it is pursuing something, or something is pursuing it. Thus, the perception in West Africa about mental illness remains a strange one. As partially noted, mental illness is a disease with a physical and identifiable course displayed through different kinds of symptoms (Mechanic, 1999). Mental illness is also a disease based on personal judgment about normal and abnormal behavior through cultural or social inclination. The psychiatrist views mental illness as an unhealthy behavior that occurs through biological, epidemiological, developmental, and social perspectives (Ibid). According to the World Health Organization and the National Institute for Mental Health, mental illness is a condition that affects the cognitive, emotion, and behavior of the individual.

On the same par, the most important types of major mental illness prevalent in West Africa include - major depression, generalized anxiety disorder, dementia, schizophrenia, psychosis, hallucination, post-traumatic stress disorder, panic attack, mood disorder, and an eating disorder. Dementia often leads to a decline in mental ability and may generally affect a person's healthy life. Most of the people with mental illness in West Africa that wander about the streets are those with a mood disorder, hallucination, and psychosis. They are often seen talking to themselves or other objects or other peoples with incoherent words. There are other mental health disorders that are not recognized or ignored as part of mental illness disorder, like ADHD (Attention-Deficit/Hyperactivity Disorder), anxiety, and anger. At this venture, we shall apply the basic research parameters to press on, digging up the relevant facts.

Background Of The Study

The negative perception of mental illness in West Africa has led to stigmatization against those diagnosed with mental illness, and it has caused physical, psychological, social, and economic abandonment to people with mental illness. The perception among immigrants from West Africa is that those with mental illness are dangerous, unpredictable, and possessed by demons. The result of the contrary opinion on mental illness leads to punishment, abandonment, confinement, denied food and treatment. Some of those diagnosed with mental illness are often chained together and asked to go about begging for money for their captures. The inhumane treatment of the mentally ill persons has led to their untimely death due to food starvation and flogging with a cane. The mentally sick persons sometimes are deprived of seeking treatment because of their restrictions by the society that they are unpredictable and can attack another person at any time.

The mentally ill persons are socially abandoned by not allowing them to interact with family members or the community. The mentally sick may be kept in the open and chained to prevent their escape. On being fastened to a tree, the mentally ill are left at the same spot both days and night to be beaten by rain, sun, and bugs. The food deprivation against the mentally ill persons in West Africa sometimes makes them escape from their family as to go out and search for food in trash bags. It is the consummation of those bad foods that leads to contamination and disease infestation – which may lead to an early demise. The mentally ill person that goes around begging for decent food from people in the community are sometimes chased away with a stick and maybe beaten with rod or stick.

The mentally ill in West Africa are denied of clothing and wander around the environment naked. Some mentally ill persons may have wounds all over their bodies caused by infections. Lack of shelter for the mentally ill also makes some of them move from one geographical location to another in search of food and care. The children also boo the mentally sick and may throw stones to them as a sign of humiliation. The children may be seen singing negative songs against mentally ill persons.

The attitudes of mental health workers are not different from those of the general public. The mental health professional stigmatizes against the mentally ill by not giving them adequate treatment. The mentally ill persons that had the opportunity to see a health professional may not get the necessary treatment or medicine to treat their mental illness. The lack of proper government policy on mental illness is another problem hampering the treatment of those diagnosed with mental illness in West Africa. Most countries in West Africa have little or no policy established mental health centers and hospitals to care for the mentally sick individuals. There are also a few diagnostic and treatment centers to diagnose and treat the mentally ill patient.

Purpose Of The Study

My research on the cultural perspectives and stigmatization against the mentally ill persons in West Africa is essential to curb the negative stereotypes, myths, and stigma associated with mental illness (Gaebel et al., 2011; Stefanovic et al., 2016; Achiga, 2016)). The negative perception of mental illness affects not only the individual diagnosed with mental illness but also the families (Kadri et al., 2004). The topic is interesting to research on as to curtail the seeming long known myths that mentally ill persons are infectious, demon-possessed, and dangerous to live in a society (Achiga, 2016). The study will also educate the people of West Africa to understand the etiology and different types of mental illness. There is a belief among West African people that the parents' sin causes mental illness, or curses, drug use, or God's punishment (Stefanovic et al., 2016; Kpobi & Swartz, 2018). Thus, this research will provide insight into the truth about mental illness.

Unfortunately, the belief of West Africans on mental illness originated from their ancestor's cultural beliefs and spiritual understanding of the whole issue. Some West African peoples believe that mental illness has a spiritual connection based on the bible encounter (Luke 4:33-37) where Jesus cast out demons from a person possessed by evil spirits. It was the question asked to Jesus by witnesses of the miracle "if it was sins of the mad man's parents that was responsible for his madness." In other words, this study will help West Africans to understand the truth that mental illness is not infectious or has to do with being demon-possessed.

This study on cultural perception and stigmatization on mental illness among West African will help to understand the impact of factors like wars, economic deprivation, migration, isolation, and cultural effects on mental illness. It is understandable that among the reasons most people from West Africa travel out from their countries to others is to seek better living abroad and for economic empowerment caused by bad governance, and harmful socio-economic factors like non-payments of workers' salaries, good hospitals, roads, and infrastructures. The lack of these social and economic factors also manifests in the form of anxiety, depression, and post-traumatic stress disorder on individuals from West African, especially those diagnosed with mental illness. For instance, one cannot expect a hungry or suffering person to behave normally.

Besides, this study will help psychotherapists to use psychotherapies that are culturally adaptable to treat mentally ill persons in West Africa. According to Potocky-Tripodi (2002), most people from West Africa diagnosed with mental illness are afraid to go for therapy due to cultural, family, and social influences that would portray them as "mad" (Mfoafo-M'Carthy, 2016). As it were, this study will inform mental health practitioners how cultural awareness, which includes - respect for the culture, the tradition and beliefs of West Africans are essential in the therapeutic process (CMHS, 1998). The study will help counselors working with West African to understand the differences or similarities in mental health understanding, diagnosis, and treatment between the Western World and people from West Africa.

This study on mental illness perceptions and stigmatization will be vital for the governments of West African countries to have a new policy on proper diagnosis, treatment, and mental health delivery. It will also help the governments in West Africa to develop a grass-roots policy that will include education and adequate training for mental health personals (Eaton et al., 2017). The grass root policy by the governments in West Africa will also help to establish mental health institutions where proper diagnosis, treatment, and adequate medicines for mental illness treatment will be disbursed (Iheanacho et al., 2015). It will help the governments in West Africa to establish mental health centers in rural areas, where there are usually more persons with mental illness. The study will enlighten the West Africans to understand other methods that will be useful to create awareness on the truth about mental illness, like the use of churches, mosques, schools, and other worship centers to dispel the negative rumors on mental illness (Iheanacho et al., 2015). It will help the government, society, and individuals to understand other methods of treating mental illness, like psychotherapy and medication. The study will equally help people from West Africa to understand and embrace other modern means of mental health treatment (Ae-Ngibise et al., 2010).

The study on cultural perceptions of mental illness in West Africa will help the government to integrate the traditional medicine healers into one body as to curtail abuses in mental illness treatment, and to ascertain the benefits of the conventional medicine. The inclusion of local medicine healers will help to improve the standard of production of the local medication, its prescription, and disbursement to the mentally ill persons (Ae-Ngibise et al., 2010. The government may be asked to partake in sponsoring the production of evidence-based traditional medicine for mental illness treatment.

On the same par, another contribution of understanding mental illness perception in West Africa will be the involvement of communities in dispelling rumors on the culturally perceived myths about mental illness that it is caused through divine punishment, hereditary, spiritual attack, drug, and magic (Kabir et al., 2004). This study will help to bring to awareness some cultural norms that are in conflict or not feasible with modern civilization today.

My research on mental illness perception and stigmatization will help pastoral counselors to understand the culture and spirituality of people of West Africa and the therapeutic process to use in counseling individuals, groups, and communities affected by mental illness stigmatization. It will also educate pastoral counselors on the diverse cultures of people of West Africa, their social norms, religious rites, and other cultural norms that cause stigmatization of the mentally ill persons. Understanding the problem associated with stigmatization will help to educate pastoral counselors to know their own biases and values, especially in working with people from West Africa. Awareness of mental illness stigmatization will also help pastoral counselors to seek justice in communities of West Africa where there are injustices.

Education is the most crucial counseling tool to decrease stigmatization (Kabir et al., 2004), so educating pastoral counselors on methods to eradicate stereotypes and negative perception on mental illness will lead to the use of appropriate intervention strategies to reduce stigmatization against the mentally ill persons in West Africa. Proper education by pastoral counselors and other mental health professionals will help to understand the mental process of communities in West Africa and how to proceed in counseling the people. It will also help to know if there are other physical or environmental factors responsible for the stigmatization of the mentally ill persons. The study of mental health perceptions will help people of West Africa to understand the causes of mental illness and learn new skills to decrease stigmatization against the mentally ill persons (Stefanovics et al., 2016). The study of mental illness perception and stigmatization among West African immigrants will also lead to more research on the impact of culture on mental illness to avoid misdiagnoses and improper treatment. This study on mental health perception and stigmatization will also help to examine how self-identity and beliefs contribute to mental illness perception among West African immigrants, and the frame of reference for mental illness treatment. The study will discuss how family dynamic and social integration and community involvement can help in fostering healing of mentally ill persons from West Africa.

The study will help in examining the behavior of mental health professionals and mental workers like the nurses, psychiatrists, and caregivers when faced with the challenges of caring for mentally ill persons. It will give mental health workers an understanding of how social discrimination affects the treatment of mentally ill persons from West Africa. The study will lead to an understanding of how bias can lead to an unhealthy lifestyle in the form of poor diets and sleeplessness among the mentally ill persons from West Africa. The study will expose how mental illness stigmatization can make those with mental illness in West Africa to hide from coming out to seek treatment and consequently cause more dangers to self.

The study will help to understand its impact on the economy of countries in West Africa resulting from stigmatization and lack of treatment of people with mental illness. Mentally ill persons in West Africa often are discriminated against from securing a job due to the notion that they are dangerous and can harm other people. It results in workforce wastage in the workplace, and eventually, a reduction in the economic growth of the country. The lack of job for the mentally ill person and not getting financial assistance from the government often leads to their wandering in the street looking for shelter and food. It is the negative perception of mental illness and denial of fundamental basic needs of human – food and housing that affect the social, psychological, and emotional well-being of those with mental illness in West Africa.

Scope Of The Study

The scope of the study was very extensive, cutting across other countries where mental illness had been understood and treated. Thus, it may sound strange that, besides our designated scope of the study, the study of this cultural perception of mental illness was equally conducted in Philadelphia among West Africans residing in different parts of the city. The age of the participants that participated in the study ranged from 30 years to 70 years and took consideration of those that were born in West Africa, and knowledgeable on mental illness perception and stigmatization.

The study participants were also from different countries in West Africa, and with a diverse cultural and religious background. The participants in the study include two pastors, a psychologist, doctors, and health care workers. The study considered the academic level in the selection of study participants. Within the noted research parameters employed in our search, it is vital to understand some research questions that guided us here, leading to the significance of the study.

The research questions

1. What have you heard or seen about mental illness in West Africa?

2. What do you think causes mental illness?

3. What are your opinion on mental illness and mentally ill persons from West Africa?

4. How are mentally sick persons accepted or rejected by cultures in West Africa and why?

5. What are the stereotypes attached to mental illness in your lifestyle and why?

6. What are your thoughts about mental illness treatment in West Africa?

7. Would you accept a mentally ill person to work or live with you?

8. Can you describe some things you like best or dislike about mental illness diagnoses and treatment in your countries?

9. Tell me what your thoughts are when someone you know reports diagnosed with mental illness?

10. How do you want mental illness treated within your culture?

11. What fears come to your mind about mental illness?

Significance Of The Study To Healthcare

The importance of the survey on mental illness perception in West Africa is that it will help to understand how stigmatization against the mentally ill person can lead to health deterioration on individuals diagnosed with mental illness. It will expose the dangers of abandoning the mentally ill person from getting adequate diagnosis and treatment. The study will also show the importance of social interaction to improve the well-being of those diagnosed with mental illness in West Africa. The study will show the importance of using social interaction in the healing process of mental illness in West Africa.

The knowledge of mental illness is undeveloped in West Africa, so the danger of stigmatization will be exposed through awareness and education. There is a segregation of family members of one diagnosed with mental illness in West Africa from marrying to another family, and this deadly and devastating situation can be avoided through proper education on the etiology of mental illness. Though the people of West Africa perceive the mentally ill persons in their culture as crazy, dangerous, and unpredictable, the study will inform the people that a mentally ill person can work, marry and socialize with other people in society. The study will help people from West Africa and sojourners to go for proper diagnosis and treatment for mental illness. The study on mental illness will also expose the myths that mental illness is infectious, and like every other sickness, it is curable.

The study is significant as it will inform counselors and clinicians to an understanding of cultural awareness in the therapeutic process, especially how culture can influence behavior. The study helps to report on the need for proper diagnosis of mental illness in West Africa because treatment can be applied. The review is essential as it encourages good government policy on mental illness in West Africa. It will also be a source of encouragement to incorporate or research further on the efficacy of traditional medicine, and for the traditional healers to form a collective body that helps to prevent abuse in treatment.

The study is crucial as it helps West African people to explore other forms of mental illness treatment like counseling and biogenic medication that can be utilized to improve the health and well-being of the mentally ill persons. The significance of the study is immense as it exposes how improper diagnosis and treatment of the mentally ill persons can lead to early death and loss of workforce that would contribute to the well-being of West African people. As it were, the ability of this monograph to have highlighted the knowledge inherent in the case at hand and in assisting society to achieve the desired results, then the significance of the study could have been totally accomplished. Hence, there is a need to review the demographic nature of the study.

Demography

Mental illness is widespread in different cultures in West Africa, especially in rural areas where poverty is also very high. The WHO estimated that mental illness is prevalent in countries with poor Gross Domestic Product (GDP), and high poverty index.

According to the World Health Organization (WHO), 40 to 60 million people in Nigeria have a mental illness like depression, anxiety, and schizophrenia (UN Africa Renewal News, 2019). It is only 10% of the estimated 40 to 60 million in Nigeria that has access to a psychiatric or mental health worker. Most of the mentally ill without mental health care are seen roaming the streets and market square begging for foods or picking food from trash bags.

In Ghana, about 2.8 million people out of a population of 25.9 million have mental illness, with only three psychiatric health centers in the country. An estimate of 97 out of 100 mentally ill persons has no mental health access in Ghana (UN Africa Renewal News, 2019). The rate of mental illness is even higher in countries that experienced civil wars and conflicts, like Sierra Leon and Liberia.

In 2015, Sierra Leon had only one functional psychiatric hospital, and the facility is in a deplorable condition. The WHO estimated that 450,000 people suffer depression in Sierra Leon, and 75, 000 suffer schizophrenia out of a population of about 7 million (UN Africa Renewal News, 2019). The reason for the high report of depression and post-traumatic stress disorder (PTSD) in countries that experienced conflicts is due to exposure to war trauma. The problem associated with a lack of job also causes the young ones to go into drug usage, which may subsequently lead to mental illness.

In Burkina Faso, 4.3% of people residing in Ouagadougou suffer major depression (Duthe et al., 2016), and the increase in the rate of major depression was associated with poverty, chronic disease, disability, drug and alcohol use and violence (Duthe et al., 2016). The surge in the number of people suffering from depression and other mental illnesses continues to increase, even in the urban areas of West Africa. In other countries in West Africa, the rate of mental illness is on the rise due to poverty and lack of treatment centers.

Mental illness care is not taken seriously in most countries in West African, so it contributes to the poor health of the people, and a hindrance to economic development (Duthe et al., 2016). The WHO recognized mental illness as a global priority and encouraged countries in Sub-Saharan Africa to increase more spending on mental health care. The West African countries have theoretically, at least, been encouraged to increase their budget in mental health care to improve the overall health of its people. Whether the plea is adhered to or not, is another thing.

Theoretical Framework

Sadly, some West African immigrants residing in the United States view mental illness as an incurable condition. This perception comes from their cultural belief that individuals diagnosed with mental illnesses, such as Bipolar and Schizophrenia are untreatable; hence pastoral counselor finds it challenging to manage mentally ill persons from this part of the world. The cultural and spiritual perceptions of these West African immigrants possess a unique challenge for pastoral counselors to work with individuals diagnosed with mental illness. It is because of this perception of mental illness that pastoral counselors should be trained to incorporate culture and spirituality into the therapeutic process, to make an impact in preventing stigmatization against the mentally ill persons in West Africa.

The theoretical framework of multi-culturalism was pioneered by Augsburger, (1986), who argued that pastoral counselors should be trained to be culturally capable of working with people from cultures like those from West Africa. The argument is that pastoral counselors should have experience in diverse cultures, to have enteropathic knowledge in caring for clients from West African cultures (Lartey, 2003). Accordingly, Lartey suggested the following:

> Pastoral counselors should go beyond mono-culturalist care to multi-culturalism so that the needs of individuals from West African cultures can be known. It is when a pastoral counselor is knowledgeable of other people's perceptions of mental illness that he will know about their social customs, religious rites, food habits, leisure activities, family patterns, gender roles, education, and housing within each group (Lartey, 2003; p.169).

It is the lack of understanding of mental illness causes that causes stereotypes against the mentally ill person from West Africa. Hence, this monograph is poised to find a solution to this cankerous cankerworm that seems to deny the dignity of mentally challenged individuals in West Africa.

There is a need for multicultural education for pastoral counselors so that they can work with clients from West Africa to dispel rumors that mental illness is incurable. The problem with stigmatization against the mentally ill person is that if not prevented, it can induce self-hatred and victimization, especially on minority groups. Pastoral counselors should be sensitive and caring to the needs of individuals with mental illness in their caseload. Pastoral counselor's multicultural education can help to encourage their clients with mental illness to understand that they have worth, value, and dignity. Another importance of pastoral counselor's teaching is that it will help them to understand their own biases, benefits, and the skills to work with clients diagnosed with mental illness. The suggestion is that pastoral counselors should be trained in multi-culturalism as to be sensitive to the needs of their clients. A pastoral caregiver needs to recognize the presence of God in various cultures and the uniqueness of oneness in humanity (Lartey, 2003).

On the same note, O' Grady, White & Schreiber (2015) talked about the need for pastoral counselors to go out and be agents of change for others, to have impacts on their lives. The change involves being courageous to go to communities and advocate for the less privileged and mentally ill persons. To be an agent of change, pastoral counselors need to be knowledgeable of their clients' culture and religion. Affective pastoral counselors should also be competing in culture and social justice that is prevalent in society through multicultural competence (Ibid). Multicultural competence also helps pastoral counselors to understand cultures and survive in counseling members of that society. Multicultural competence involves being knowledgeable about how social injustice is affecting the disadvantaged. Pastoral counselors' understanding of the social and cultural identity of the people they serve is essential as to be committed to the eradication of social injustices, and help people understand that they are equal irrespective of their age, gender, age, and cultural orientation (Ibid).

Consequently, O'Grady, White & Schreiber suggested thus:

> The use of multicultural counseling inventory can be used by pastoral counselors to have knowledge, beliefs, and attitudes to counsel their clients with mental illness. It is essential for pastoral counselors and other counselors to know their biases before advising a client as to avoid countertransference. Pastoral counselors should also have cross-cultural experiences for personal development and professional effectiveness (O'Grady, White & Schreiber, 2015).

The multicultural experience involves exposure and engagement with diverse cultures to be a competent pastoral counselor. As against the background of the Igbo aphorism, "when a blind person leads the way, there is the possibility for both the leader and led to falling into a pitch".

No wonder then, Leong & Kim, (2001), suggested that pastoral counselors, other counselors, and supervisors should learn how to use intercultural sensitizer as an educational tool. Leong and Kim also said that educational counseling training models are beyond attitudes and beliefs but knowledgeable about specific people's cultures. They contended that when pastoral counselors are not knowledgeable about the people's culture, it leads to frustration, but proper knowledge leads to better intervention strategy. The study highlights that good experience in the value system of different cultures helps counselors to identify potential problems and solutions to apply (Ibid). The study also calls for increased training of pastoral counselors to have a broad knowledge of cultural sensitivity and skills to work with cultures in West Africa. The report also said that the training of counselors would help understand if they have any biases toward minorities that may require referring the client to another counselor. The article also argued that educating counselors on cultural sensitivity will help them to understand the values and lifestyles of clients from a different culture in West Africa (Ibid). It is appropriate to understand the differences between religion and individual behavior when working with a client to use appropriate intervention strategies. The article also argued that acquiring knowledge of cross-cultural sensitivity involves using one's cognitive and behavioral process to understand the client.

On a different but unique note, Yang & Lu (2007) suggested the need to develop universal psychology that will advance an understanding of indigenous cultures through three levels:

- Empirical research,

- Philosophical reflection, and

- General construction.

They argued that these three procedures would help to analyze the mental processes of people in a given culture. Yang and Lu also see human personality as a manifestation of consciousness with different levels of identity, such as supreme to identity and egoistic consciousness. There are factors that influence human behavior such as the environment, family members, friends, communities, and the world (Ibid). Cultures and religion mark the social evolution that shapes own state of consciousness and an individual-oriented culture that leads one to follow one's own learning, while the corporate-oriented culture that values compassion, altruism, and societal harmony leads to transpersonal bond (Ibid).

Eventually, Riedel-Pfaefllin & Smith (2010) explored how differences in social and historical experiences, languages, culture, and beliefs can shape our being. It emphasizes that collectedness determines our family and that human beings evolved through different cultures, finance, social, and political orientations. The effect of poverty and violence should be treated seriously by pastoral counselors, and the problem of war, famine, and other forms of abuse can lead to anger, but there are calls for forgiveness. It is the knowledge of these problems that call for intercultural competence among pastoral counselors when counseling clients from other parts of the world. There is a need for pastoral counselors to use intercultural dialogue when working with people from different cultures so that they can listen and talk together. The intercultural dialogue will also help counselors to develop an in-depth understanding of diverse cultures and the ability to make good choices in treatment modality (Ibid). Forgiveness should also be used by pastoral counselors to heal wounds caused by traumatization in different cultures.

On another note, Melinda & Sharp (2017) contended that post-colonializing as an African practical theology should be part of pastoral counselors care training for the health and transformation of communities. It says that surrounding one's name, creed, and culture alone may be a hindrance to development. Melinda and Sharp argued that post-colonializing theory of change is for improvement, and to attain greater height by pastoral counselors. They call pastoral counselors to be agents of change in some of the colonial systems that have paralyzed communities from development and an equitable relationship among its citizens.

Supportively, Van Beck (2010) argues that pastoral training and education are necessary to bring about wholeness in rural services. This wholeness is essential through personal cross-cultural experience. The study emphasizes that cross-cultural interactions are rooted in an encounter as exemplified by Jesus Christ's encounter with people. It is in this view that pastoral counselors' goals should focus on the wholeness of the client and the community they serve. The rural meeting is rooted in speaking the truth in love and not to be abusive or manipulative (Ibid). Pastoral ministers are meant to be forgiving and imitate Jesus Christ's caring attitude to people. The cross-cultural experience goes beyond the therapeutic but to that of the spiritual, especially when pastoral counselors are willing to work for other cultures.

According to Lartey (2003), the issue of globalization, internalization, and indigenization started through a multicultural experience. It is through multicultural expertise that we can talk about internalization or globalization, and indigenization which can occur through a holistic approach (Op. Cit., Beck, 2010). The article acknowledged that pastoral counselors might face different cross-cultural challenges, but it also helps them to understand people's priorities, personalities, and presuppositions (Ibid). Pastoral counselors should be aware that care for their clients should also be on the eradication of social injustices. It is also vital for pastoral counselors to know that in counseling others, they need their own self-evaluation, self-criticism, training, and willingness to follow the code of ethics.

Hitherto, cross-cultural counseling is the manifestation of multicultural pastoral care, and the stronger the counseling skill, the better the empathy (Ibid). Multicultural pastoral care can improve the relationship between a client and the caregiver, between different groups seeking care and in the relationship between larger communities. Multicultural awareness by pastoral counselors can increase wholeness in larger cities through excellent therapeutic skills. Through multicultural teaching, knowledge people are empowered to learn new skills, it is necessary to train pastoral counselors to have multicultural skills to work in larger communities that are different from the European and American model of education. The multicultural counselors need to be holistic in their approach and able to take care of their clients' needs (Ibid).

Similarly, Koramoa, Lynch & Kinnair (2002) contended that professionals working in a multicultural society should be sensitive to cultures that cause harm and those that are beneficial in enhancing a child's cultural identity. The study encourages professionals to understand that their responses can promote a positive outcome or cause injury if inappropriate interventions occur. They (Koramoa, Lynch & Kinnair (2002) equally argued that every culture has its own belief. In other words, professionals should know those cultures in order to make appropriate decisions.

The multicultural theoretical framework will help pastoral counselors to understand the culture and spirituality of people of West Africa and the therapeutic process to use in counseling individuals, groups, and communities affected by mental illness stigmatization. The multi-culturalism framework will also educate pastoral counselors on the diverse cultures of the people, such as social norms, religious rites, and other cultural norms that cause stigmatization of the mentally ill persons. Educating pastoral counselors on multi-culturalism helps counselors to know their own biases and values, especially in working with people from other cultures. With multicultural awareness, pastoral counselors can seek justice in communities of West Africa where there are injustices.

Education is the most crucial counseling tool to decrease stigmatization. Thus, educating pastoral counselors on multiculturalism will lead to the use of an appropriate intervention strategy to reduce stigmatization of the mentally ill persons in West Africa. Good multicultural education by pastoral counselors helps them to understand the mental process of communities in West Africa and how to proceed in counseling the people. It also helps to know if any physical or environmental factors are responsible for the stigmatization on mentally ill persons. Multicultural teaching will help people of West Africa to learn new skills to decrease stigmatization on the mentally ill persons. However, having dwelt extensively on the parameters and related facts on the topic at hand, there is every need to expound what others have observed on our perception, in chapter two.

CHAPTER TWO

REVIEW OF RELATED LITERATURES

The search for the literature reviewed articles on the cultural perception of mental illness by West African immigrants being focused on their cultural understanding, the opinions, stigmatization, treatment, spirituality, government policies, interventions, and barriers to treatment, may not be as numerous as one would expect. Thus, by our literature reviews, digging to understand what other studies that had, in one way or the other, discussed the issue of mental illness and to give credence to those researchers are uphill tasks. As it were, the approach applied here using the literature review search was to go from the databases to the journals, to general knowledge, and academic search and ultimately published materials. All the same, as a general scientific approach in monographs of this magnitude, the use of words in such undertakings is of paramount importance, hence, the present setting.

Keywords Used In The Research Study

1. "Mental Illness" - It is an abnormal behavior from normal behavior which may include: inappropriate nudity, aggressive behavior, harmful behavior, expressive language, and interpersonal relationship that is unacceptable to society.

It is also a disorder in the brain that can affect a person's behavior;

2. "Evil Spirit" - It is a demonic possession or the association of physical and spiritual un-cleanliness (Matthew 8: 28-34; Luke 9:37-43);

3. "Curse" - A word spoken to invoke a supernatural power, inflict harm or punishment on someone or something else;

4. "Stigmatization" - The devaluation of an individual or exclusion of someone from some social interaction, even those that meet the criteria, and may result in social, psychological, emotional, and physical harm. It is also a mark of disgrace, shame, and dishonor on a person or something;

5. "Witchcraft" - The practice of magic or the use of spells or divination to vulnerable people or sorcery to produce unnatural effects in the world. It is also the manipulation of the demonic host through incantation and casting of spells (Luke 16:26);

6. "Perception" - The state of being aware of something through discernment, realization, awareness, understanding or intuition;

7. "Dangerous" - What can cause harm or injury to a person or thing.

8. "Madness" - It is a state of having an abnormal state of mind or derangement;

9. "Religion" - From its 2 Latin verb roots derivation, *'religio'* (obligation, bond, or reverence) and *'religare* (to bind), that

is, the way of binding on what one considers as bond or obligation. It equally refers to a group that has particular meaning and value attached to their lives;

10. "Spirituality" – Is a sacred life of a person, object, or a principle of an individual to show reverence to God. Academically, spirituality incorporates the minutest activity of a human being.

Framework of the Literature review

According to the World Health Organization (WHO, 2001), mental illness affects 10% of the adult population and 25% of all individuals at a time. The WHO reported that the prevalence of mental illness is very high, and by 2020, depression will be the leading cause of mental illness. In West Africa, the rate of mental illness is very high due to wars, unemployment, lack of treatment facilities and lack of professionals to care for the mentally ill patients (Atindanbile & Thompson, 2011). The WHO also reported that African countries spend less than 1% of their health care budget on mental illness and its treatment (Read, Adibokan & Nyame, 2009).

The burden of mental illness is very high in West Africa, and an effort to address the problem is not yielding a positive result (Omar et al., 2010). The concentrations of the little resources approved for mental illness treatment are in the urban areas, thereby making the rural areas vulnerable to more mental illness challenges (Read, Adibokan & Nyame, 2009). It is a lack of mental health workers, the stigma on mental illness, and inadequate financial resources allocated to mental disease that leads to failure to address mental health issues in West Africa (Omar, Op. Cit).

Numerically, West Africa is a sub-region in Africa that has many cultural beliefs on mental illness, and there is a need to address the problem of mental illness in West Africa as it leads to human wastage, stigmatization, and even untimely death of the mentally ill persons. The countries in West Africa are Benin, Burkina Faso, Ivory Coast, Gambia, Ghana, Guinea, Guinea Bissau, Liberia, Mali, Mauritania, Niger, Nigeria, Senegal, Sierra Leone, and Togo. The immigrants from these West African countries, especially those residing in Philadelphia, have the same negative perception of mental illness like those in West Africa. Most immigrants from West Africa continue to abide by their cultural ideology on mental illness. It is the cultural belief of West African on mental illness that leads to misconceptions and misconstrued attitude to people diagnosed with mental illness, and there is a similarity in the culture of West Africa countries on mental illness. There are also problems of stigmatization, myths, and stereotype among the cultures in West Africa. The states of West Africa may differ in language, religion, and tradition but have a similar view or perception of mental illness. Some of the mental health challenges faced by immigrants from West Africa are due to stressors from relocation, discrimination, religion, social, and psychological stresses with loss of intimacy with family members and friends. There is also no psychotherapy in most West African countries to counsel the mentally sick.

Perceptions

Ultimately, individuals, professionals influencing the beliefs and attitudes toward mental illness, and cultural perspectives of different cultures are so many (Stefanovics et al., 2016). This culturally constructed belief system is evident among most West African residing in Philadelphia, who view mental illness as being caused by evil spirits (Achiga, 2016). Some West Africans believe that mental illness is a curse by God (Stefanovics, Op. Cit). The beliefs by West

African on mental illness have resulted in the stigmatization of those diagnosed with mental illness, and hindrances to their mental health treatment (Ibid). Achiga, (2016), on the other hand, contended that some doctors in West Africa also believe that substance abuse, evil spirit possession, hereditary, traumatic events, shock, spells, or God's curse on a person are serious contributors to the problem at hand. There is a contention by Akan people in Ghana that culture influences people of West Africa and the perception of mental illness diagnosis and treatment (Opare-Henaku, 2013). Their supernatural belief about mental illness influences the perception of mental illness among the Akan people, and it has formed their health-seeking behavior on mental illness (Ibid). The evil understanding of mental illness by some religious groups also leads to abuses like restraining with chains, food denial, seclusion, and degrading treatment (Osafo, 2016). Klik et al., (2019), on the same point, contended that it is the societal identification and perception of mental illness that decide on how to navigate the help-seeking process. The identification of mental illness and the symptoms often determine the eagerness of the mentally sick person to seek treatment (Klik et al., 2019).

There is also a belief among some West Africans that mental illness is infectious and should be avoided to prevent others from being infected (Achiga, (2016). It is this belief and stigmatizing attitude by some Nigerian doctors with regards to mental illness that make access to treatment difficult. Achiga (2016) stated that some Nigerian doctors think that mentally ill persons are dangerous and can harm others (Jack et al., 2015). There is the perception by some religious groups that mentally ill persons are different from other persons and should not mingle with healthy individuals (Osafo, 2016). There is a belief that those with mental illness are the cause of their disease, so they are not pitied (Corrigan & Watson, 2002). The homeless individuals are perceived as mentally sick, unwanted, and are excluded from their family members (Asante et al., 2016). Another perception is that the mentally ill homeless individuals are those that disobeyed their family and are receiving punishment from God for their disobedience (Ibid). The effects of these negative perceptions against mental illness may lead to humanizing torture of mentally ill persons, and confirmation of the advice that seeking medical treatment by the mentally sick is a waste of time (Read et al., 2009), and may affect health-seeking behavior of those with mental illness (Osafo, 2016). These beliefs by some Nigerian doctors also that mental illness is a curse that makes it difficult for mentally ill patients to get treatment in hospitals or have a conversation with family members and friends. There are often misconception and miscommunication between a mental illness patient and a mental health worker that is unfamiliar with the culture of the patient which may lead to the inability of clinicians to have a sound therapy (Al-Krenami & Graham, 1997). It is essential for clinicians working in West Africa to know the content of what the patient means by symptoms of an illness to understand how a patient sees the world through cultural knowledge (Al-Krenami & Graham, 1997).

Mental illness perception is the negative thoughts or ill feelings about individuals diagnosed with mental illness by others, groups, or society. The impression may be culturally or individually based and most often leads to stereotypes and discrimination in the areas of employment, housing, food, and medical benefits (Manning & White, 1995). The stereotypes in the media that mentally ill persons are dangerous to make them not to get married (Egbe et al., 2014). The quality of life (QOL) for sick mentally persons depends on the attitude shown by mental health workers – the psychiatrist, nurses, record clerk, and other health officials during initial intake (Bello-Mojeed & Ogunsemi, 2016; Olusina & Ohaeri 2003) contended that the mentally ill patients who are well treated could express satisfaction with their quality of life (QOL) and sense of well-being. The sick, mentally persons treated can also realistically talk about their personal qualities, strengths, and weaknesses of their socio-cultural issues. There is a need for social interaction and a non-judgmental attitude to the mentally ill as to alleviate the emotional, social, and physical components associated with discrimination (Bello-Mojeed & Ogunsemi, 2016). The impact of societal stigma against the mentally ill person in West Africa calls for the mental health workers not to be judgmental in treating the mentally sick persons, as to dispel the rumors that mentally ill persons are dangerous (Egbe et al., 2014). The report is that the negative perception and stigmatization against the mentally ill persons in Nigeria starts from childhood age to adulthood in the form of social distancing (Oduguwa, Adedokun & Omigbodun, 2017). The issue of negative perception and stigma against the mentally ill is a universal phenomenon seen across race, ethnicity, age, groups, and religious organizations (Bella-Awusah, Adedokun, Dogra & Omigbodun, 2014).

The Pentecostal clergies perceived mental illness as a diabolical interference in the life of a person (Onyina, 2002), and the perception leads to the use of deliverance or exorcism for the cure of mental illness (Onyina, 2002; Asamoah, Osafo & Agyapong, 2014). The argument is expressed by Ae-Ngibise et al. (2010) that mental illness is demonology connected. The traditional belief in West Africa is consistent with the same view as the Pentecostals that mental illness is associated with demon possession (Asamoah, Osafo & Agyapong, 2014). Sodi 2009; Kpobi & Swartz, 2018) also contended that West Africans cultural belief is that physical and spiritual problems, ancestral, and evil spirits and spells or curses cause mental illness (Monteiro & Balogun, 2014). The negative perception leads the mentally ill from Ghana to seek treatment with traditional medicine men whose belief is shrouded with supernatural ideas that mental illness is a punishment from God (Kpobi & Swartz, 2018; Makanjuola et al., 2016).

Stefanovics et al., (2016), on the other hand, in studying the attitude, fear and behavioral intention towards mental illness in five countries of Brazil, China, Ghana, Nigeria, and the United States found no correlation between supernatural beliefs in mental illness and the bio-psychosocial aspect of mental illness. The study found that people have different perspectives on mental illness due to their culture. Stefanovics et al., (2016), in support of the argument, concluded that cultures like Nigeria believe that mental illness is caused by evil spirits or the work of God.

There is a report that mental illness affects about 10% adult population at any moment and 25% of all individuals at a time in pupils' life (WHO, 2001; Yendork, Kpobi & Sarfo, 2016). In Ghana, the perception is that mental illness is a spiritual illness caused by human sorcery, evil spirit, and Supreme Being (Yendork, Kpobi & Sarfo, 2016), and it is responsible for the type of treatment the people sort. Walker (2015) reported that mental illness accounts for 14% of the global burden of disease that can lead to other conditions.

Stigmatization

Stigmatization is one of the problems experienced by mentally ill persons in West Africa and not to seek treatment (Liegglio, 2017). In children and youths, stigmatization results in shame and diminished self-esteem, which, leads to loss of productivity and strained relationship with others (Ibid). One of the things that come to mind in any contact with the mentally ill persons in West Africa is that they are worthless, and the perception often leads to loss of confidence for the future on' the mentally ill person (Corrigan & Watson 2002). The effect of the stigma may result in a patient's anger because of the prejudice against the mentally ill persons. The self-stigma experienced by the mentally ill persons might cause them to have low self-esteem (Corrigan & Watson 2002).

The stigmatization of those with mental illness has been in existence since the history of man, and it creates fear in people which also leads to the exclusion of the mentally ill from society (Gur et al., 2012). The caregivers assigned to the mentally ill persons are often socially segregated as they may not move and interact with other people comfortably, and family members are sometimes aggressive or abusive to the mentally ill person (Ae-Ngibise et al., 2015). The issue of mental disability also impacts negative consequences to both the individual and their caregivers or friends in West Africa (Ibid - Ae-Ngibise et al., 2015). The burden of the negative experiences on mental illness includes the overall physical, psychological emotions, and the financial cost of taking care of the mentally ill person (Ibid- Ae-Ngibise et al., 2015). It is the burden of caring for the mentally ill person in West Africa that leads to abandonment of the sick mentally, and subsequent exacerbation of their mental illness (Ibid- Ae-Ngibise et al., 2015). The problem of segregation against the mentally ill and their caregivers call for support to eradicate stigma and provide financial support to families of those with mental illness (Ibid- Ae-Ngibise et al., 2015).

The issue of stigma against the mentally ill often leads to socially undesirable behavior and social discrimination (Tawiah et al., 2015). According to the World Health Organization (2012), most people with mental illness experience stigma and discrimination, and the stigma reduces the mentally ill person from whole to one with low social rank and devalues them in the society (Gyanfi, Hegadoren & Park, 2018). Other forms of stigma against the mentally ill person that might result in prejudice against others in West Africa include – embarrassment, rejection by others, and loss of socialization with others in the neighborhood (Liegglio, 2017).

Treatment stigma is another form of discrimination against mentally ill persons in West Africa (Egbe et al., 2014), and it affects their overall health-seeking behavior. The addition of social, psychological, and economic burden of stigma causes low self-esteem, isolation, unemployment, social anxiety, housing problems, and poor social support (Egbe et al., 2014).

The mentally ill persons in West Africa experience stigmatization and discrimination due to misconceptions about mental illness generally, and it creates a gap between the sick mentally person's needs and availability (Dako-Gyeke & Asumang, 2013). The segregation or discrimination against the mentally ill in West Africa shows the need to include programs that will empower those with mental illness in socioeconomic programs, and to protect their rights (Ebuenyi et al., 2018). The social stigma against the mentally ill persons also contributes to the anger experienced by the mentally sick persons (Corrigan & Watson, 2002). Stigmatization is a universal phenomenon noticeable across race, ethnicity, age, group, and religious organizations, and it comes through social distancing (Bello-Awusah, Adedokun, Dogra & Omigbodun, 2014). Kadri et al. (2004) argued that stigma against the mentally ill person is noticeable in most countries of the world, especially in West Africa.

Alas! Those countries in West Africa with low income often experience more stigmas against mentally ill persons due to low priority accorded to mental illness treatment (Dako-Gyeke & Asumang, 2013), and the stigma affects both the mental health officials, the families and also the mentally ill patient (Barke, Nyako & Klecha, 2011; Dako-Gyeke & Asumang, 2013). In Nigeria, there is a report that family members reject 17.5% of those with mental illness; and 72.2% said that they would not work for people with mental illness (Ebuenyi et al., 2018). The stigmatization against the mentally ill persons is a sign of ignorance, fear, lack of knowledge, and superstition, and may result in harassment, violence, and dislike of mentally ill persons (Dako-Gyeke & Asumang, 2013). Again, Barke, Nyarko & Klecha (2011), supported the notion that stigmatization is a serious problem that affects the patient, families, and mental health institution taking care of the mentally ill person, and the stigma can also be directed to mental health care professionals (Jack et al., 2015).

The reason given for the unemployment of those with mental illness is for safety reasons to prevent others from been attacked if there is a relapse in the health of a mentally ill person (Ebuenyi et al., 2018). Picco et al., 2016; WHO, 2001) contended that stigma occurs across cultures and comes in the form of shame, rejection, discrimination, stereotypes, and separation. The issue of stigmatization often makes the mentally ill persons not to seek treatment, and it can cause the sick mentally person sickness to become chronic (Gur et al., 2012). Stigma also is seen as a barrier between the religious groups and the mental health treatment team in the treatment of mentally ill persons (Osafo, J. (2016). Stigmatization against the mentally ill in West Africa goes with denial of the basic necessity of life like food, housing, and clothing, and also the denial of jobs and education (Dako-Gyeke & Asumang, 2013). The fear of relapse by those with mental illness and cultural beliefs are factors that often make employers un-desirous to hire a mentally ill person (Ebuenyi et al., 2018).

Due primarily to the stigma attached to mental illness, Mfoafo-M'Carthy, Sottie & Gyan (2016), contended that it is the media portrayal of a mentally ill person as dangerous, crazy and unpredictable that tends to create more stigmatization and hindrance to the treatment of the mentally ill persons in cultures like Nigeria. The mentally ill are stereotyped as dangerous, incompetent, and unable to help themselves (Corrigan & Watson, 2002). The media also portrays the mentally ill persons as a homicidal maniac that can kill, rebellious, and who behaves like a child (Corrigan & Watson, 2002). There is a report that the use of chaining is to keep the mentally ill person safe from escape by families and a way of treatment and punishment for bad behavior (Read, Adibokan & Nyame, 2009).

The fear that the mentally ill person is homicidal might result in keeping them outside the house, while other people make decisions on their behalf (Corrigan & Watson, 2002). The mentally ill persons also are physically abused by beating them with a stick or given them overdose medication as a punishment (Robert, 2001). It is the alienation, stereotype, social withdrawal, discrimination that is the major self-stigma, and the intervention to decrease the self-stigma should be focused on these problems (Brohan et al., 2011). Also, a current diagnosis of depression on bipolar persons, and the age of onset of treatment are responsible for self-stigma of the mentally ill person in some cultures in West Africa (Thome et al., 2012).

The mentally ill person's perception of the illness comes through self-stigma, anticipated stigma and discrimination, perceived discrimination, and lack of knowledge on the real disease itself (Gyanfi, Hegadoren & Park, 2018). Shame can make a mentally ill person to be in a state of grief, and may induce hopelessness and helplessness, and affects the recovery of the mentally ill person (Tawiah et al., 2015). There is a specific knowledge that the diagnosis of mental illness often leads to mood instability, increased hospitalization, poorer physical and psychological outcomes, and decreased psychosocial functioning (Ritsher & Phelan, 2004; Thome et al., 2012; Gyanfi, Hegadoren & Park, 2018). Stigma is also known to diminish the quality of life and impede social integration (Tawiah et al., 2015). Most people with mental illness in West Africa are even discriminated against by family members, the community, and even health care workers (Brohan et al., 2011). The discrimination against the mentally ill persons in West Africa comes through denial in getting a job, education and health care (Gyanfi, Hegadoren & Park, 2018; Watson et al., 2007) and it makes the mentally sick to live a life of fear, guilt, isolation, and segregation. Mental health issues often have an impact on individuals and their families through financial, social, and health burdens (Tilahum et al., 2017). The social responsibility of mental illness in children relates to their inability to associate with others, while the financial burden relates to families' inability to pay for mental health treatment (Tilahum et al., 2017). Stigma makes the mentally ill person seem as if he or she is different from others, and it impacts educational attainment, employment, and housing (Liegglio, 2017). The problem of stigmatization against the mentally ill person in West Africa often results in loss of self-esteem and self-efficacy (Watson et al., 2007). The effect of the external and internal stigma could lead to depression and deterioration of mental illness in the mentally sick individuals from West Africa, so reducing stigma is essential to improve the health of the mentally ill (Egbe et al., 2014). The prejudice against the mentally ill person in West Africa might result in the withdrawal of services like employment and health care services (Corrigan & Watson, 2002). The family members of the mentally ill in West Africa are often discriminated against by others because of the mental illness (Kadri et al., 2004; Gureje et al., 2005), and family stigma usually has a psychological effect on children with mental illness (Liegglio, 2017). There is also a report that children with mental illness are often discriminated against by their siblings (Liegglio, 2017).

According to Makanjuola et al., 2016, there is a high perception of self-stigma in individuals diagnosed with mental illness across cultures, and the stigma is more among high school and college students in Ghana. Mentally ill persons in West African countries also experience stigmatization, social rejection, and isolation by mental health workers and laymen (Yendork, Kpobi & Sarfo, 2016; Picco et al., 2016). The stigmatization against the mentally ill often leads to low self-esteem, social abandonment, poor quality of life, unemployment, and rejection (Barke, Nyarko & Klecha (2011), and they are stigmatized as devalued members of society (Picco et al., 2016). The best way, often to feel safer to avoid prejudices, discrimination, and stigma by people with mental illness is to hide it from caregivers and others (Liegglio, 2017).

The stigma against the mentally ill is more pronounced in rural areas as compared to those in the urban areas (Makanjuola et al., 2016) or overseas where they are readily taken care of. The issue of stigmatization against the mentally ill is less with higher education. Stigmatization affects the mentally ill person's participation in private and public life (Gaebel et al., 2011). In terms of public life, the mentally ill person discriminated against manifest in a reduced societal network and devalued self-esteem. The mentally ill persons from West Africa also experience discrimination at workplaces, in public business, which results in societal withdrawal and secrecy (Gaebel et al., 2011). The internal stigma has been found to reduce an individual's sense of hope and self-esteem, which may result in depression and social avoidance (Picco et al., 2016). The internal stigma results in poor psychosocial outcomes and reduced quality of life for persons with mental illness (Picco et al., 2016). The effect of stigma often leads to hatred of the mental health workers by the mentally sick person who sees them as not doing much to assist them in getting better. The stigma against the mentally ill person in West Africa can come through the nurses treating those diagnosed with mental illness or through violation of their human rights, unemployment, and lack of housing (WHO, 2012).

There is a high incidence of discrimination against the mentally ill persons in South Western Nigeria (Adewuya & Makanjuola, 2008) through social distancing, and the incorporation of anti-stigma education as the way out of this stigmatization is essential. Stigmatization in West Africa means disliked, a disgrace and embarrassment to the society, and it is the stigma that ruins the quality of life of the mentally ill and excludes them from good things of life (Gur et al., 2012). Many people in West Africa do not disclose their mental illness due to the common threat that will not protect their confidentiality; instead, it brings stigma against them (Kushitor et al., 2018). The bases of the stigma against the mentally ill persons are on the notion that they are dangerous, violent, and untreatable (Adewuya & Makanjuola, 2008), and stigmatization is a hindrance to the treatment of those diagnosed with mental illness. Ritsher and Phelan (2004) reported that stigma causes harm to people diagnosed with mental illness, and the internalized stigma represents the most significant form that leads to high depressive symptoms and reduced self-esteem. The depression experienced by a mentally ill person, in turn, leads to alienation, stereotypes, low self-esteem, and social withdrawal (Ritsher & Phelan, 2004). The mentally ill persons are sometimes abused in Ghana through sexual molestation, flogging, denial of education, insults, and forceful in early marriage (Aremeyaw, 2013; Asamoah, Osafo & Agyapong, 2014).

The two types of stigmatization against the mentally ill are the felt or perceived stigma, and the enacted discrimination (Tawiah et al., 2015). The felt or perceived stigma is the real fear of social discrimination against a mentally ill person, while the enacted perception is the practical experience of discrimination in jobs because of mental illness (Tawiah et al., 2015). The mentally ill persons also experience structural discrimination in social, political, and legal decisions, and often result in concealment of mental illness from partners, relatives, and employers to avoid rejection (Barke, Nyarko & Klecha (2011). There is also a report that a third of the mentally ill persons are stigmatized against after treatment and discharged in Ghana by family members refusing to accept them back in the family (Barke, Nyarko & Klecha (2011). The best way suggested in dispelling rumors and stigmatization on mental illness in West Africa is through education (Achiga, 2016).

Interventions and Treatment Strategies

Osafo, J. (2016) reported that only 2% of those with mental illness seek treatment while 98% are untreated, and there is a wide gap in mental illness treatment between low income and middle-income countries in West Africa. Abdulmalik et al., (2014) identified low government policy on mental health as one of the issues hindering mental health treatment in West Africa, and due to the existence of non-government organizations to improve, mental health in West Africa. Kim and Salyers (2008), however, contended that educational and emotional support for families in caring for their beloved ones with mental illness is essential. Lack of knowledge, financial burden, and lack of family interest are identified as some barriers to mental illness treatment in West Africa (Kim & Salyers, 2008). Other problems identified as a hindrance to mental illness treatment in West Africa include inadequate funding, misconceptions about mental health, stigmatization, lack of human resources to treat mental illness, and human abuses (Abdulmalik et al., 2014). It is reported that economic standing may predict an individual's sense of psychological distress, as high income decreases psychological distress (Kushitor et al., 2018). The lack of resources, stigma, burnout, and high cost of mental illness treatment contributes to hindrances in mental illness treatment (Kim & Salyers, 2008).

The treatment of mental illness in West Africa is also through the psychiatrists, the traditional and spiritual healers (Roberts, 2001). Some spiritual healers also incorporate traditional healing methods to treat mental illness in West Africa (Roberts, 2001). The incorporation of the conventional healing method with the clinical practice may be a good step in the healing of a mentally ill person (Lefley, 1990), and the intervention will be more acceptable when clinicians collaborate with family members in the healing process of a mentally ill person. There is a perception that more professionals and mental health workers alike, the psychiatrists, social workers, and psychiatric nurses can be utilized to provide care to mentally ill persons in West Africa, and lack of these health workers are the reason for chaining the mentally ill or the use of overmedication by traditional healers to treat the mentally ill person (Jack et al., 2015).

The high percentage of untreated people with mental illness calls for collaboration between mental health workers and religious groups to improve mental illness treatment provision to the grassroots, and enhance funding for mental illness treatment in West Africa (Osafo, 2016). It is reported that due to a lack of human resources and stigmatization, only 1 in 5 mentally ill people is treated with mental health issues in Anglophone countries in West Africa (Abdulmalik et al., 2014).

The demonization of mental illness as caused by evil spirits by religious groups and health personals are some hindrances to psychiatric ill-treatment in West Africa, so there is a need for collaboration to address it (Osafo, 2016). Stigma against mental illness in West Africa is one of the reasons education is needed to dispel the negative rumors on mental illness that demons or evil spirits cause mental illness (Gur et al., 2012). Educating the people of West Africa on mental illness will assist in removing their misinformation about mental illness (Gur et al., 2012). The use of education that starts from an early age is one of the best ways to fight stigmatization against mentally ill persons. The fight should begin by using children and the youths in the fight against mental illness discrimination (Bella-Awusah, Adedokun, Dogra & Omigbodun, 2014).

The use of children's education in the battle against mental illness will make them share the experience and knowledge with their families and society (Rahmen et al., 1998). Oduguwa, Adedokun & Omigbodun supported the use of school-based education or intervention in mental illness treatment, and they contended that governments in West Africa should partner with mental health professionals to have a method where students will be allowed to partner with the mentally ill person as to decrease the negative perception on mental illness. The teachers will be of utmost importance in the fight against the stigmatization of the mentally ill people in West Africa (Gur et al., 2012). Teachers will also be aware of their prejudices against the mentally ill persons before undergoing to educate school children on misconceptions about mental illness in West Africa (Gur et al., 2012).

Guraje et al., (2006) contended that the best way to reduce stigmatization against the mentally ill persons in West Africa is through education on the nature and causation of mental illness. It is lack of knowledge on the etiology of mental illness that causes deep-rooted negative attitude on mental illness in West Africa, but education increases positive attitude on mental illness (Guraje et al., 2006). The strength of some developing countries in West Africa is the ability to handle major mental health illness in their respective states with the scarce resources in their disposal and family willingness to rehabilitate the mentally ill person (Lefley, 1990). Some countries in West Africa might merge their indigenous healing method with the scientific modalities, and integrate the support of the family member in the healing process of people with mental illness (Lefley, 1990).

Sometimes, mental health professionals are not helping to have a collaborative relationship with families of a mentally ill person, so the education of mental health workers on how to understand the cultures of families of a mentally ill person is necessary (Kim & Salyers, 2008). The use of education will help to inform people from West Africa that mental illness is treatable, and that they should have the mindset to seek for treatment. Education is an essential factor in influencing people's health outcome, so higher education will assist in lowering psychological distress and improving people's way of life (Kushitor et al., 2018). Also, educating families about mental illness is essential as it will assist in enhancing the relationship between family members and the mentally ill person (Kim & Salyers, 2008). The utilization of psycho-education and community involvement is proper to de-stigmatize mental health symptoms and decrease fears about mental illness (Shannon et al., 2015). Although there is poverty in third world countries, like those in West Africa, the family members still attend to the needs of their people with mental illness (Lefley, 1990). Some immigrants from West Africa, regardless of their orientation, even recognize the importance of herbs and symbolic rituals in the healing process (Lefley, 1990).

There is a perception that people who view mental illness as caused by bio-psychosocial factors have less stigmatization against the mentally ill than those who believe in the supernatural cause of mental illness as "evil spirit," "curse" and "demonic manipulation" (Guraje et al., 2006). Stigma may not be the only reason mentally ill persons in West Africa do not seek treatment, but it might be due to past trauma (Shannon et al., 2015). Also, the mentally ill person's unwillingness to seek treatment may be due to a lack of information on mental health services available in their community, and the perceived cultural norms about mental illness (Shannon et al., 2015). It is also believed that culture influences people individual's behavior, attitude and action on mental illness, and people who experienced structural trauma or stigma are fearful of discussing their mental illness in public and may not seek treatment (Shannon et al., 2015).

Kyei et al., (2014) examined the relationship between depression, anxiety, somatization, wellbeing, and spirituality to know if there are more benefits in using the localized intervention that uses spirituality and cultural beliefs in the treatment of mental illness in Ghana, and found that there was no relationship between depression, anxiety, somatization and spirituality to mental illness treatment. It was found, however, that most people favor spiritual intervention to mental illness treatment in West Africa (Kyei et al., 2014).

There was a positive change in knowledge and attitude against the mentally ill after the education of children was used in some countries (Pinfold et al., 2003). The education program against myths on mental illness should be a gradual process of using literacy programs to increase awareness of mental illness (Bella-Awusah, Adedokun, Dogra & Omigbodun, 2014). The education program will demystify mental illness and reduce the issues of mistrust, fear, and stigma against the mentally ill person in West Africa (Kabir, Iliyasu, Abubakar & Aliyu, 2004). Achiga, (2016), added that the best way to dispel rumors and stigmatization on mental illness is through education. Rahman et al., (1998) contended that school mental health education program or awareness is successful in improving mental health awareness, and the children can share their understanding of mental illness with their parents. The mental health awareness program can be beneficial in rural areas to increase community knowledge of the mental illness. The school setting is an excellent place to access students, families, and community mental health needs and address the educational needs and wellbeing of the mentally ill persons (Atiola & Ola, 2016). The school setting helps to access untreated mental health problems among school-aged children and adolescents. The school-aged program is undeveloped in West Africa, but it will be useful to circumvent the social and economic barriers that hinder mental illness diagnosis and treatment (Patel et al., 2013; Atiola & Ola, 2016). The school-aged setting will also help to take the children away from depending on the traditional models of assessment and treatment of mental illness in West Africa.

The use of church ministers for health education and social support is another way to treat the mentally ill person from West Africa (Asamoah, Osafo & Agyapong, 2014) and it reflects the caring part of religion. Akotia et al. (2014) reported that religion plays a significant role in the life and cultural perception of mental illness among people from West Africa. It is the culture and religion that influences West African people's attitudes toward suicide or mental illness (Akotia et al., 2014). The use of faith in mental health treatment increases self-esteem, hope, lower anxiety, and suicide thoughts (Asamoah, Osafo & Agyapong, 2014). The belief among most people from West Africa is that God is the controller and owner of life, and whatever happens to a person has a spiritual force behind it (Akotia et al., 2014), and it is through prayer or commitment to God that mental illness gets cured. Some pastors in Ghana use beating, chaining, and prolonged fasting as a way of cure for mental illness but it was deemed unacceptable by other religions (Atindanbila & Thompson, 2011; Ofori-Atta et al., 2010; Asamoah, Osafo & Agyapong, 2014). Spirituality in West Africa is another institution that provides moral and social motivation for people, so training religious leaders will promote positive health for mentally ill persons in West Africa (Osafo, 2016). It is, therefore, necessary for proper collaboration between mental health workers and religious groups to address abuses against the mentally ill persons, which had been a barrier to mental illness treatment in countries like Ghana (Osafo, 2016).

Kpobi and Swartz (2018), contended that due to the high cost of the biomedical form of treatment of mental illness, and the limited number of trained mental health workers, people in Ghana look for an alternative method of treatment that focuses on socio-cultural beliefs for treatment – the traditional medicine men. About 2% of those diagnosed with mental illness in Ghana seek biomedical therapy while the rest of Christians and Muslims use the conventional, and faith healing for treatment (Yendork, Kpobi & Sarfo, 2016). The faith healing form of therapy involves praying to cast out demons assumed to be the cause of the mental illness (Ae-Ngibise et al., (2010). The religious belief and the cultural perception on the purpose of the mental illness are mostly responsible for the type of treatment the mentally ill person sorts (Yendork, Kpobi & Sarfo, 2016).

The involvement of the media outlet, churches, students, and laypersons in the education program is another way to end the negative perception of mental illness in West Africa. The creation of community-based services, provision of financial services, and improving collaboration for mental health delivery could be used to improve mental health services in West Africa (Bukola et al., 2019), also an appropriate knowledge on mental illness is essential for the community program to succeed in mental illness treatment (Kabir, Iliyasu, Abubakar & Aliyu (2004). It is also vital to understand people's culture, norms, and beliefs in determining the health-seeking behavior and treatment of mental illness in West Africa. It is ignorance and stigma that hinders the cure of the mentally ill persons in Nigeria. Iheanacho et al., (2015), added that though biological and other factors may lead to mental illness, improving access to psychiatric health care in countries such as Nigeria can help prevent mental illness, like post-natal depression among women. James, Igbinomwanhia & Omoaregba (2014), also suggested that the incorporation of the clergy in the identification and delivery of mental health in Nigeria would improve mental health awareness and treatment. Waterman et al., (2018) suggested the use of cognitive-behavioral therapy (CBT) psycho-education to treat depression and anxiety in Sierra Leon which has proved effective in improving mental health functioning within the United Kingdom adult population.

Policy

Abdulmalik et al., (2014) acknowledged that it is the low government policy on mental health, and lack of knowledge that are the problems confronting mental health issues in the five Anglophone countries of West Africa, Nigeria, Ghana, Liberia, Sierra Leon, and the Gambia. Tilahum et al. (2017) contended that 10 to 20% of children worldwide experience a mental health problem, and it affects their lives and those of their families. Ebuenyi et al., 2018 reported that mental illness has continued to be a problem in low and middle-class countries of West Africa due to poor socio-economic, political, and social welfare policies of the affected countries. The treatment gap between the low and middle-income countries in West Africa ranges up to 90% due to the lack of mental health workers and health facilities (Tilahum et al., 2017).

It was observed that unemployment and stigma are some of the issues encountered by a mentally ill person, and it affects their lives (Ebuenyi et al., 2018). Walker (2015) contended that good government policy in the area of financial resources, education, infrastructure, and human rights protection would go a long way in reducing stereotypes against mental illness in Ghana. The barriers that influence unemployment of the mentally ill include lack of education, stigma, or discrimination by employers and poor government policy on mental illness (Ebuenyi et al., 2018). The West African countries should follow the same pattern of investing in good mental health policy, especially in financial and human resources. It is the pitfall in the area of financial investment and mental health workers that hinder progress in mental illness treatment (Walker, 2015; Omar et al., 2010). The policy that would assist in improving the lives of people with mental illness in West Africa is to improve access to evidence-based care, and respect for the rights of individuals (Patel et al., 2010). The policy will involve the joint involvement of governments, mental health professionals, and civil society, communities, and families to decrease mental illness in West Africa (Patel et al., 2010).

The problem of depression experienced by reproductive women in West Africa also calls for the governments to establish more mental health clinics and train mental health workers on how to recognize depressive symptoms (Coleman et al., 2006). The use of psychotherapies like Cognitive Behavioral Therapy (CBT) and medication regimen, should be introduced in primary health centers in West African communities (Coleman et al., 2006). The villages and traditional healers in West Africa should be educated on depression causes and treatment modalities as some reproductive women seek treatment with traditional healers where the depressive symptoms may not be recognized (Coleman et al., 2006).

The problem identified with psychiatric service in Ghana is that of chronic underfunding and mismanagement, which is not able to match the agreed standard of the nations on health care and human right (Robert, 2001). It is a lack of accountability in the health sector of countries in West Africa that is responsible for the poor management of the mental health sector. There are problems with management and policy, and violation of people's rights and safety is high, but nobody will speak out due to fear of victimization (Robert, 2001). The lack of proper procedures for patient's admission, review or discharge is observed in some mental illness facilities in West Africa, and it often results in patients being in the hospital for months without being assessed (Robert, 2001). The lack of proper government policy is responsible for making mentally ill persons seek treatment with quacks, traditional healers, or not seeking treatment at all (Walker, 2015). The inadequacy of the public health sector in Nigeria, for example, is responsible for the poor knowledge of mental illness disorder and stigma also which contributes to the poor treatment given to the mentally ill person (Gureje & Lasebikan, (2006).

Another problem identified as responsible for the inadequate treatment of mental illness in West Africa is corruption. It is corruption that makes funds approved for mental illness not used for its purpose in West Africa. The mental health hospitals in West Africa are not getting adequate funding, which results in poor infrastructure to diagnose and treat mental illness, and might result in people traveling long distances to get treatment.

The burden of mental health in poor urban communities may grow due to migration from the rural areas, and it may worsen their quality of life if not addressed by the governments in West Africa (Kushitor et al., 2018). The use of social cohesion may be used in the community to bring about a sense of belonging, ability to help one another, mutual trust, and communication with one another to improve the quality of life of those with mental illness (Kushitor et al., 2018). There is a call by a community-based mental health to establish legislation in poor and middle-income countries in West Africa to monitor human rights abuses against mentally ill persons (Read, Adibokan & Nyame, 2009). This human right will also be used to prohibit unlawful maltreatment, degrading treatment, or punishment against the mentally ill person (Read, Adibokan & Nyame, 2009).

Mental illness is considered of low priority in West African countries because of the government focus on the eradication of poverty, so the Mental Health and Poverty Project (MHAPP) can be utilized to evaluate and implement mental health policies in West African countries (Omar et al., 2010). The people of West Africa residing in poor neighborhoods and lack financial needs may also develop psychological distress that may result in mental illness (Kushitor et al., 2018). The involvement of the civil society organization (CSO), was suggested to play an important advocacy role on mental illness issues, and to change the negative attitude on mental illness in West Africa (Omar et al., 2010). International policy stakeholders may also be sought on areas of finance to create mental illness awareness in West Africa (Omar et al., 2010).

Osei et al., (2012) reported that mental illness represents 9% of disease burden in Ghana, and women are mostly affected. According to the WHO (2003) report, the prevalence of mental illness is very high, and by 2020, depression will be the leading mental health problem in the world (Atindanbile & Thomson, 2011).

The governments in West Africa should train and use community volunteers or village-based health workers in each local government to inform people about mental illness (Eaton, Nwefoh, Okafor, Onyeonoro, Nwaubani & Henderson (2017). The mental health Gap Action Program (MHGAP) introduced by the WHO is a tool for use by a non-specialist in mental health to deliver treatment for disorders like depression, schizophrenia, and dementia (Patel et al., 2010). The program aims to bring mental health treatment to cover the entire population, especially in poor and middle-income countries of West Africa. The federal governments in West Africa should involve the State and Community Mental Health Program (CMHP) clinic in the dispensation of mental illness awareness to the populace, especially in local communities where the rate of mental illness is high (Eaton, Nwefoh, Okafor, Onyeonoro, Nwaubani & Henderson (2017). The government policymakers should allow psycho-education to be in the school curriculum to inform the people about mental illness (Asamoah, Osafo & Agyapong, 2014) and the collaboration between mental health professionals and the church on mental health management and treatment (Yendork, Kpobi & Sarfo, 2016). The utilization of education to reach children and mothers in rural communities would help them identify mental illness early and seek treatment (Tilahum et al., 2017). Also, lack of government and stakeholders' support in coordination and supervision of mental illness are responsible for the poor treatment of mentally sick individuals (Tilahum et al., 2017). The utilization and success of the MHGAP program rest in the commitment of the government to use stakeholders at all levels in mental illness eradication (Patel et al., 2010). A hindrance to mental illness treatment in West Africa is the short time training of mental health workers, poor content of mental health education, and inaccessibility of mental health centers (Tilahum et al., 2017). Family education is essential in the care and rehabilitation of mentally sick members because of cultural interdependence (Lefley, 1990). The involvement of families has been recognized as strength to understand the patient more and aid in their healing (Lefley, 1990).

In support of the argument on mental illness perception, Biswas et al., (2016) contended that governments in West Africa should help to train more health workers to achieve better health for the mentally ill persons. They suggested that psychiatrist perception of mental illness across cultures varies, and understanding of this variation in West African countries helps in the treatment of mental illness. Biswas et al., (2016) also supported that there is a tendency for cultural biases when a psychiatrist is sent to a different culture to treat the mentally ill individuals. Onyencho, Omeiza, Wakil (2014) maintained that the government in West Africa, non-governmental organizations (NGOs), and health care providers could assist in the treatment of the mentally ill person and post-traumatic stress disorder (PTSD) in West Africa. It is the non-support by the governments in West Africa in mental illness treatment that made some families use chaining to keep a severely mentally ill person in a place (Read, Adibokan & Nyame, 2009). There is a need to address the negative cultural rooted attitude of chaining a mentally ill person through adequate funding of mental illness services in West Africa.

The use of media campaigns by the government can be a substantial contributing factor to the awareness of mental illness services in West Africa (Eaton, Nwefoh, Okafor, Onyeonoro, Nwaubani & Henderson (2017). Mfoafo-M'Carthy et al., (2016), therefore, suggested that the issue of stigmatization can be reduced through media outlets in countries like Nigeria and Ghana, as to reduce the negative attitude attached to mental illness. The use of anti-stigma programs in the local, national and global campaigns, the schools, health care workers, and the police, and media outlets can be successful in reducing mental illness stigma (Gaebel et al., 2011). The use of the campaign strategy for awareness and enlightenment has been effective in lowering stigmatization in 25 countries when combined with a variety of approaches (Gaebel et al., 2011).

Mentally ill persons were reported to have experienced violence and other human rights abuses from the police and other law enforcement agencies during post-war Liberia (Kohrt, 2015). There is no law to protect the mentally ill persons in low and middle-income countries of West Africa, so there are calls to enforce a bill that will help enforcement agents and mental health workers to collaborate in the prevention of sick mentally abuses (Kohrt, 2015). The use of anti-stigma programs to increase awareness of the mental illness and decrease stigma, as suggested in South Africa, might be useful in West African countries (WHO, 2012). The anti-stigma campaign should include the government and non-governmental organizations, and it should consist of the youths, health care professionals, teachers, politicians, schools, journalists, religious groups, pharmacists, stakeholders, police, and the media to discourage stigma (WHO, 2012; Kohrt, 2015). The mental health clinicians should also learn how to implement anti-stigma programs, and family support, advocacy groups could be used to advance mental health policy, legislation and funding in West African countries (Kohrt, 2015).

The World Health Organization (WHO), also suggested that early education through the media (Newspapers, Televisions, Radio, Arts, Brochures, and Pamphlets) can help to reduce stigma, and for the people of West Africa to understand mental illness. The governments in West Africa are called to rebuild mental health centers and social welfare programs, which would be utilized to assist in mental illness treatment (Kohrt, 2015). The establishment of a crisis intervention team (CIT) is also an excellent way to enforce mental health safety, reduce stigma, and direct mentally ill persons to treatment centers (Kohrt, 2015).

According to Adejoh, Temilola, and Adejunwon (2018), the right motivation by family members and mental health rehabilitation offices can help drug abusers diagnosed with mental illness to improve. The evidence points out that positive perception and reinforcement are associated with mental illness recovery. The caring and empathizing with clients diagnosed with mental illness in West Africa often leads to healing from the inside (Adejoh, Temilola, and Adejunwon, 2018).

The community mental health workers (CMHW) should be trained to understand the mental health job and be consistent with the health demand of their mental health patients in their communities (Agyapong et al., 2015). The community mental health worker should also learn how to deliver psychiatric health care at the community level to decrease stigma and discrimination (Tilahum et al., 2017). There is a suggestion that the CMHW in West Africa should learn how to dispense psychotropic medications during training due to the shortage of quality mental health workers. It is the shortage of quality mental health workers that is responsible for the inadequate health care provision in rural communities in West Africa (Agyapong et al., 2015). The WHO also estimates that lack of mental health professionals is responsible for not getting quality health care needs in low and middle-income communities in West Africa and the reason for high patronage of traditional and religious healers (Agyapong et al., 2015). It is estimated that 650,000 people in Ghana are suffering from a severe mental health disorder, while 2,166,000 are suffering from moderate to mild mental health disorders (Agyapong et al., 2015). There is also a suggestion that mental health training should be the responsibility of the psychiatrist alone, but community health care workers should be trained to assist in poorer countries like Ghana to assist in dispensing medicine and improving mental health care (Agyapong et al., 2015).

Puckree et al., (2002) contended that many people in West Africa do not know about psychotherapy, so mentally ill persons patronize traditional healers, and it calls for the mental health officials to integrate westernized practice with conventional methods to promote healing for mental illness. Lack of profound knowledge about mental illness causes and prevention is also responsible for West African people's attitude on mental illness, as was the case in HIV transmission and prevention (Green, 1999). The need for cultural explanation is more pronounced in rural areas of West Africa where there are strong traditional beliefs, so good government policy is essential for the people to understand the causes and treatment of mental illness (Quinn, 2007). There is a perception that referring the mentally ill persons to mental health professionals for counseling can be useful to reduce stigma and increase wellness (WHO, 2012). The use of the legislation can be utilized to prevent stigma in West Africa, and the media can monitor to ensure that mental illness information is accurately mentioned to lessen fear. The use of effective advocacy on mental illness is necessary to reduce stigma against mentally ill people in West Africa, and the support should involve the participation of mental health professionals, families, key stakeholders, and policymakers on mental health treatment (Abdulmalik et al., 2014).

Causes

Lund, Meyer, Stein, William & Flisher, (2013), reported that low income in cultures like Nigeria is the cause of mental illness and also people's inability to have resources that improve health. Owitti et al. (2015) argued that psychological distress, such as intense anger, worry, guilt, stress, bereavement, and grief, can lead to mental illness. Owitti et al., (2015) also maintained that social factors such as lack of housing, financial difficulties, marital problems, and interpersonal issues might lead to mental illness.

Lack of education, poverty, and unemployment are cited as the primary cause of mental illness in Ghana (Osei et al., 2012). Pigeon-Gagne et al., (2017) reported that chronic poverty and unstable environment could lead to mental illness, and socioeconomic factors may contribute to mental illness (Hadley et al., 2008). The mental health challenges experienced by most West African countries are also linked to civil wars, unemployment, and AIDS epidemic, with few mental health professionals to assist in controlling the problem (Atindanbile & Thomson, 2011). Hadley et al. (2008) contended that infants of mothers with mental illness disorder have more behavioral issues than those whose mothers have no mental illness disorder. Depression is also a common mental health disorder in women from West Africa due to unfortunate socio-economic situations and gender (Coleman et al., 2006).

Furthermore, maternal depression, poverty, and stressful life can contribute to the development and mental illness (Hadley et al., 2008). Other causes of depression in reproductive women in West Africa are associated with infertility, divorce, and widowhood, which also threatens her womanhood and resource security in her house, family, and community. The stress experienced by reproductive women in weak rural areas of West Africa adds to their inability to maintain steady food supply to the family or pay for their housing, and it adds to their depressive symptoms (Coleman et al., 2006). Some women in West Africa use their reproductive capacity to have more children as a social tool and resource security, with the notion that the children will grow up to support the family. It is the women's eagerness to maintain security in West Africa that also leads to stress and depression (Coleman et al., 2006).

The mental health of homeless adolescents in Ghana are found to be twice more than the youths in society (Asante et al., 2016), and it is caused as a result of the number of years they have been on the street, the substance use, stigma from family and community, suicide ideation, and physical and sexual abuse (Asante et al., 2016). The stressors encountered through migration from one region to another during wars, violence, and political upheaval in some West African countries may result in mental illness (Bukola et al., 2019; Shannon et al., 2015). The mentally ill may also experience anxiety of being attacked, stigmatized by others, or the problem of language barriers issues in a new environment (Bukola et al., 2019). The effect of war often leads to post-traumatic stress disorder (PTSD) and major depression (Shannon et al., 2015). The use of drugs is reported to cause psychological distress, which may also lead to depression (Asante et al., 2016). It was also reported that youth's mental health deteriorates due to poor psychological functioning, and the effect of stigma leads to loneliness, social alienation, and depression (Asante et al., 2016). It is contended that the influx of people from rural to urban is leading to more mental health disorders like depression in Ghana (Kushitor et al., 2018).

Mak, Chong & Wong (2014) stated that it is the belief among countries outside of the western world like Nigeria that evil spirits, curses, or ethical violations cause mental illness, and it leads to stigmatization and shame to both the mentally ill individual, and their families. Other caused identified as responsible for mental illness include, alcohol, drug use, divine punishment, evil spirit, and trauma (Kabir, Iliyasu, Abubakar & Aliyu, 2004), and the symptoms manifest through aggression, talkativeness, eccentric behavior, and wondering. It was found that substance abuse is the primary cause of mental illness for men in Ghana, while women reported more depression and anxiety (Osei et al., 2012). There is a belief among West Africans that psycho-cultural thinking, religion or spiritual beliefs, social difficulty, cognitive impairment, disaster, economic hardship, substance abuse are some of the causes of mental illness (Monteiro & Balogun, 2014). The people of West Africa recognize psychosis through unusual behavior, and depression and anxiety manifest through negative emotions (Monteiro & Balogun, 2014).

Akotia et al. (2014) maintained that it is the external forces that enter a person that causes mental illness like psychosis.

There is a report that women in Ghana relate the cause of their mental illness to poverty, childcare, infertility, witchcraft, and discrimination as a result of the aging process (Osei et al., 2012), and those seeking for mental illness treatment in Burkina Faso are those that have developed recurrent condition like major depression (Pigeon-Gagne et al., 2017). The men in Ghana diagnosed with mental illness may seek treatment at the psychiatric hospitals, but women prefer to seek treatment at churches or shrines or with their primary care providers for physical health issues (Osei et al., 2012). The lack of family support, limited access to mental illness facilities, and stigma can worsen mental illness in West Africa (WHO, 2012).

Traditional Healing

The conventional practice is the belief and practices recognized by communities to provide healthcare to its people (Kpobi, Swartz, Omenyo, 2018). The practice involves using community known methods of healing which is peculiar to the communities in West Africa to achieve wellness (Kpobi, Swartz, Omenyo, 2018; Onyina, 2002; Asamoah, Gyadu, 2013). The traditional healers are utilized more for healing in West Africa due to cultural beliefs and values, and it leads to health-seeking behavior (Kpobi, Swartz, Omenyo, 2018). The traditional healers provide holistic care that involves social, cultural, and emotional needs of West African peoples' understanding of mental illness (Kpobi, Swartz, Omenyo, 2018). There is a report that about 70% to 80% of people with mental illness in West Africa use traditional medicines to treat mental illness first (Opare-Henaku, 2013), and some people believe that mental illness healing is better with the conventional medicine than the modern psychiatric approach (Asuni, 1990).

Most people diagnosed with mental illness seek treatment first with traditional healers, the priest, spiritualist, or herbalist before taking the biogenic medication (Ibrahim et al., 2016). The reason for the first use of traditional medicine to treat mental illness in West Africa includes – availability, affordability, and accessibility (Ae-Ngibise, 2010; Opare-Henaku, 2013), and lack of knowledge or attribution of mental illness to supernatural belief (Barke, Nyarko & Klecha (2011). Another reason for consulting traditional healers in West Africa is because the consultation is free from stigma (Roberts, 2001). Sometimes, it is the fear of shame and the poor mental health treatment that makes the mentally ill person hesitant to seek treatment (Ibrahim et al., 2016). In most of the West African countries, mental illness is often of low priority, and they have few mental health workers and facilities to provide intervention (Ibrahim et al., 2016). The notion among mentally ill people in West Africa is that traditional healers can understand mental illness through a cultural perspective (Ibrahim et al., 2016). The conventional healers also understand how mental illness diagnoses affect the family and the mentally ill person, and they try to establish a social code that will bind the family and the community together through culture (Roberts, 2001). It is also the culture of West African on mental illness that often results in poor clinical outcomes for mentally ill persons in the later years (Ibrahim et al., 2016).

The traditional practice utilized in treating a mentally ill person in West Africa sometimes use fetish ritual, and their healing methods lack standard or scientific explanations (Nwoko, 2009). The mode of treatment used by traditional herbalists often makes their treatment suspicious and untrustworthy, but some people see their treatment as affordable and an alternative to western medication. The mentally ill person and a family member are sometimes made to live with the traditional healer, who uses herbs and recitation of incantations as part of their healing process (Asuni, 1990). Some conventional healers use voodoo to treat the mentally ill clients (Nwoko, 2009), and it shows the need to incorporate the traditional healers into a specific functional group. The incorporation of the conventional healers into one body will assist in emphasizing the healing power of using herbs for mental illness treatment (Nwoko, 2009).

There are three types of traditional healers in West Africa – the herbalist, the spiritualists, diviners' faith healers, and the regular birth attendant (Atindanbile & Thomson, 2011). The herbalists use herbs from the environment for the treatment of the mentally ill persons, and other traditional healers may use herbs, plants, and animals to cure the sick (Kpobi, Swartz, Omenyo, 2018). The herbalists sell their products in the market and may ask their clients to avoid particular food or sex before taking the herb (Atindanbile & Thomson, 2011). Sometimes, the traditional healers keep the mentally ill person in their compound where they are made to do chores or engage in farming (Asuni, 1990). The spiritualists/diviners use divination to diagnose their client's mental illness causes and proclaim that they get their healing powers from the Supreme Being, lesser gods, or the ancestors (Osei, 1994; Atindanbile & Thomson, 2011). The diviners may use divination and communicate with deities to cure the mentally ill person (Kpobi, Swartz, Omenyo, 2018). Some traditional healers abuse their mentally sick clients by handcuffing them, denying them food for a long time, or by beating and burning (Robert, 2001). Some mentally ill persons in West Africa got blinded because of chemicals put in their eyes by traditional healers to stop the client's hallucination or some chemicals dropped on their ears to auditory hallucinations (Robert, 2001). The problem accounted for in using the traditional healing method in West Africa is that the right to decide, appeal, or reject a treatment is determined for the mentally ill person by another person (Robert, 2001). Some psychiatrists are made to incorporate the traditional belief of the people's culture in the healing process because of what the people believe (Robert, 2001).

The faith healers use religion or prayer to heal their mentally sick clients. They use the event of the Pentecost as "speaking in tongues," holy water, and may combine traditional religion and indigenous practices like singing, dancing, and other spiritual healing methods to cure their mentally ill clients (Osei, 1994; Atindanbile & Thomson, 2011). The religious or spiritual healers may use exorcism, holy water, prayers, fasting and prophesying, anointed oils, and salts for healing. The traditional birth attendants acquire their training of healing through family members or relatives or by spiritual gifts (Atindanbile & Thomson, 2011; Kpobi, Swartz, Omenyo, 2018), and they can help in the treatment of psychosis and depression.

The traditional healers also use herbs for the treatment of the mentally sick person in West Africa (Asuni, 1990). The mentally ill are sometimes restricted from moving out from the family compound to prevent their escape, and they do chores like farming (Asuni, 1990). In some cases, the religious houses that are involved in the treatment of the mentally sick use physical restraints to prevent the mentally ill in their captivity from escape, and some are tied with ropes in both hands, ankles, and backs to prevent escape (Asuni, 1990). The mentally ill person may be asked to go around, asking for alms, singing, and dancing in the street (Asuni, 1990). The family members of the mentally sick may also be allowed to participate in the healing rituals of their sick ones.

Ae-Ngibise et al., (2010) explored the difference between the traditional healers and the faith healers and contended that the traditional healers use libation and herbs to treat the mentally ill persons, while the conventional faith-based healers use prayers, fasting, and holy water to treat the mentally sick person (Puckree et al., 2002). There is a suggestion that the government in West Africa should promote collaboration between the traditional and biomedical healing methods to improve the wellbeing of those with mental illness (Ae-Ngibise et al., 2010). It is emphasized that the social, economic, and cultural factors are responsible for the more extensive use of traditional and faith healing methods of treating mental illness in West Africa (Ae-Ngibise et al., 2010). The shortage of mental health professionals in West Africa is also responsible for the flocking of mentally ill persons to the traditional healer (Atindanbile & Thomson, 2011). The spiritual effect is believed by some West African culture as the causative reasons for mental illness and influences the reason the mentally ill persons flock to patronize the traditional healers (Tanner, 1999; Ae-Ngibise et al., 2010). The conventional healers also show social and psychological support to their clients that lead to more mentally ill persons to flock to them.

The factors that make the mentally sick to go for traditional and faith-based treatment are their availability, inadequate biomedical medications, and lack of mental health staff to treat the mentally ill persons in West Africa (Ae-Ngibise et al., 2010). The psychiatrist is one to 1.4 million people in Ghana, while the traditional healers are one in 200 people (Ae-Ngibise et al., 2010). The poor people's inability to afford the biomedical treatment makes the mentally ill persons go to the traditional healers whose costs are cheaper and affordable. The regular healing practice in West Africa is rooted in their old belief (Summerton, 2006).

Atindanbile & Thomson, (2011) contended that 80% of people from Africa prefer to patronize the traditional healers because of their belief that western medicine is right for physical illness, but powerless against supernatural causes of mental illness. The idea is that sickness of emotional or psychological natures are a punishment from gods for evil, and western medicine is helpless towards the cure. The people of West Africa believe that western medicine gives temporary relief to cure mental illness, so the preference for local herbs and indigenous medication for treatment. The traditional drugs are also cheaper and affordable for the mentally ill person to buy and accessible without traveling for extended miles to be found (Ae-Ngibise et al., 2010; Atindanbile & Thomson, 2011; Sodi et al., 2011).

According to Osei (2001), there is a need to assess the efficacy of the traditional healing method in healing the mentally sick persons. Osei encouraged the need to train the conventional healers in therapeutic limits and to refer clients they cannot treat to others (Osei, 2001), and learn scientific methods of diagnosing and treating the mentally ill persons (Atindanbile & Thomson, 2011). The traditional medical counsel can be established and used in West African countries to regulate the work of traditional healers ((Kpobi, Swartz, Omenyo, 2018).

Religious/Pentecostal Healing

The people of West Africa do not rush to seek mental illness treatment for emotional issues, preferably the first thing they do will be to seek help with the clergy, family members and friends, people for social and psychological problems (Senreich & Olusesi, 2016). Most of the people from West Africa do not know about psychotherapy treatment but think about mental illness as a spiritual issue. Sometimes, the mentally ill persons are physically restrained by their religious healers through handcuffing or by using iron metals to hold the mentally sick ankle (Asuni, 1990). In psychiatric hospitals, the mentally ill person may be sedated to prevent him or her from escaping, but it infringes on the patients' rights (Asuni, 1990). Some people from West Africa believe that psychosis is a brain issue caused by spells, voodoo, demonic possession, and the best way is to treat it spiritually (Senreich & Olusesi, 2016). Religion and spirituality are perceived to contribute to healing, though it has not stayed away from irregularities and neglect inpatient care (Elkonin, Brown & Naicker, 2012).

The new method of healing the mentally sick person in West Africa is through prayer in churches. The concept of this modern deliverance method of healing came from the bible encounter (Luke 4: 33-37), where Jesus cured a mad man possessed by demons. The bible narrated that the insane man was possessed by "evil spirits," lived in a cave and wandered about in the hillside, and it is the same perception people from West Africa have about the mentally sick person as being mad and possessed by evil spirits. The bible recorded that Jesus used the power in the word of God to deliver the "mad man" after asking him "how many they are," and the response from the mad man was that they are legions. The concept of spirituality in healing is to help individuals with mental illness to find, seek, and use their own life to improve health (Elkonin, Brown & Naicker, 2012). The use of religion or spirituality in mental health healing leads to reverence, wonder, piety, and unconditional love of God in religion or philosophy (Elkonin, Brown & Naicker, 2012).

The concept of healing a person with mental illness started with the new era of Pentecostalism and Charismatic groups in the church. The Pentecostal and Charismatic are those that believe in the power of using the Holy Spirit, as mentioned in the bible to heal the sick. The belief is that being baptized in the Holy Spirit gives the person the ability to tread upon serpents and scorpion, and nothing shall hurt them. The concept related to the Pentecostal gift as was given to the disciples of Jesus Christ at Pentecost to go out in the world preaching the word of God and healing the sick or those possessed by evil spirits. The Charismatic and Pentecostal members in the church are men and women with the gift of healing or performing miracles, and implore the word of God to cure those with mental illness. The people from West Africa perception is that mental illness is possession by "demon" and deliverance comes through the prayer of exorcism, using the word of God, calling the blood of Jesus Christ, using anointed oil or holy water and other approved church methods that healing of those with mental illness can occur. They believe among West African also is that "demons" hear the word of God, and by a command from an anointed man of God, the devil departs from those possessed by evil spirits.

The current belief in the Pentecostal and Charismatic method of healing has helped to change the health-seeking behavior of those with mental illness that prayer can work wonders in curing mental illness. Other religious groups are taking a clue from the Pentecostals and Charismatic to apply their own methods of healing those with mental illness. There is a need for the inclusion of religion and spirituality for mental illness treatment since the majority of people in West Africa accept it as a positive way of mental illness cure (Senreich & Olusesi, 2016).

There is a need for governments in West Africa to introduce a policy that will increase access for mental health care, stop mental illness discrimination, and use informal consent before treating a mentally ill person (Ibrahim et al., 2016). The government should also improve mental health services in all communities where people live in their country as the inability to seek mental illness treatment might lead to lower quality of life (Ibrahim et al., 2016).

Table 1: Literature Review Article Summary

CAUSES	PERCEPTIONS	STIGMATIZATION	TREATMENT	POLICY
a. Evil Spirit	a. Mad	a. Avoidance	a. Education	Train community health workers.
b. Drugs	b. Idiot	b. No job	b. Funding	
c. Curses	c. worthless	c. Denied treatment	c. Grassroots outreach	
d. Hereditary	d. Crazy	d. Social avoidance	d. Traditional healing	More media involvement.
e. Trauma	e. Useless	e. Structural avoidance	e. Prayer of exorcism	Good legislation.
f. Spell		f. Restrained with chain	f. Biogenic Medication	
g. shock		g. Poor social support		
		h. Denied education		
		i. Abandoned		
		j. Flogging		
		k. Sexual molestation.		

Figure 1: Literature Review "Cultural Perceptions of mental Illness in West Africa"

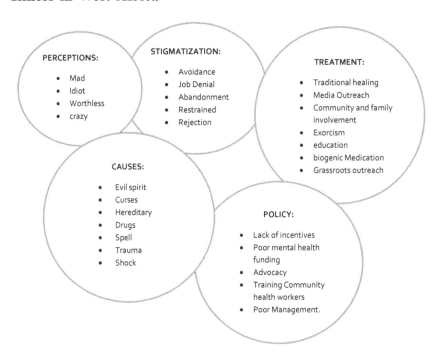

CHAPTER THREE

METHODOLOGY

Inevitable Introduction

As one could vividly see from the writing of this thesis, the methodology adopted for it - this academic work was essentially anchored on its nature and objective. The research scientifically appealed to various agencies and bodies, in one way or the other, connected with the mentally sick individuals, digging very deep to find the root cause of the problem and attempting to proffer key solutions to it. Therefore, our approach to the issue might not be as traditional as one would expect, thereby underlying the originality of the monograph. Thus, the study on the cultural perception of mental illness by West African immigrants in Philadelphia utilized the qualitative method and multicultural theoretical framework to understand the lived experiences of those diagnosed with mental illness in West Africa. The study helped to understand the myths, prejudices, and stigma against those diagnosed with mental illness in West African countries. It also exposed how a lack of treatment facilities and poor government policy on mental illness can affect the wellbeing of people with mental illness in West Africa.

The study used stories from individuals and families from West African countries to understand the problems encountered by the mentally ill person in their respective cultures. The study also emphasized the health-seeking behavior of people with mental illness, ignoring biogenic treatment but instead seeking treatment with quacks or traditional healers who are unaware of proper diagnoses and treatment of mental illness. The study was designed to change the negative perception by people from West Africa that mental illness is caused by "evil spirit possession" or curses from their ancestors, wicked people, or curse from God. The study will help to encourage persons with mental illness in West Africa to seek proper treatment, and for the government of countries in West Africa to have a good policy that would be utilized to improve the wellbeing of the mentally sick.

Design of the Method

The study design utilized an ethnographic understanding and cultural belief systems sampled from people of West Africa to understand mental illness perception. It involved in-depth interview and observation of people from West Africa, their reactions and understanding of mental illness at the moment.

The ethnographic qualitative research method used systematic methods to study people's culture through interaction or observation, and the study used participant's personal views and experiences with mentally ill persons from West Africa to narrate their experiences. The approach tries to capture West African people's reactions to mental illness diagnoses, treatment and social interaction with the mentally ill individuals. The method also exposed responses by family members, communities, and their society on mental illness, and their lived experiences of those with mental illness.

The tough interview process was through a one-on-one basis with people from different cultural backgrounds in West Africa and a focused group interview. A thorough observation of how participants responded to questions on the cultural perception of mental illness in West Africa was recognized. The use of the ethnographic study helped to understand the numerous cultures of people from West Africa and how it relates to mental illness perception. An open-ended interview method was employed to question participants on their understanding of mental illness in West Africa so that they could discuss in detail their opinion on mental illness in West Africa.

In using the narrative approach, the participants used for the in-depth interview were able to give an account of their observations and interaction with those diagnosed with mental illness in West Africa, and their personal viewpoint on mental illness. Most of the participants in the study believed that evil spirit possession or curses cause mental illness. Another observation from interviewing the participants was that people avoid the mentally ill persons in West Africa because they are seen as unpredictable and can be dangerous to associate with others. Also, family members of those diagnosed with mental illness did not want to be known as to avoid being discriminated against also by society. The observation is that cultural perception of mental illness causes the stigma and social avoidance of mentally ill persons in West Africa.

Participants

The participants that participated in the study were those born and lived in West Africa before migrating to the United States. The study participants were also those that observed or experienced mental illness problems and perception in West Africa.

Participant Inclusion Criteria

The participants that participated in the study were those born and grew up to observe mental illness perception in West Africa themselves. The participants' ages ranged from 30 years to 75 years and have observed someone with mental illness in their community in West Africa. The mentally ill person participants were expected to have observed were those already diagnosed and manifested symptoms of mental illness in West Africa. The participants were also expected to know about the mentally ill person's behavior and family or societal reaction on the mentally sick individual.

The inclusion criteria utilized were on the participant's ability to narrate their own experiences or observations on people with mental illness in West Africa. Also, the educational attainment of each participant was holistically and specially considered on their being able to speak English and communicate vividly about mental illness perception in their own culture in West Africa. The participants that participated in the study included two pastors and a Catholic priest, who had been, occasionally consulted for prayers by family members of the mentally sick persons. The belief among some West African people is that demons and evil spirit possession cause mental illness, so the tendency by some families at first value would be to take the mentally ill person to a man of God for prayers. Sometimes, as a matter of secrecy, mentally ill persons' families may take their ill person to a spiritualist or other religious groups for prayers first, to avoid public awareness of the issue in their society. The participation of the religious or spiritually oriented individuals in the study helped to understand further the perception of mental illness by pastors in West Africa.

The Muslims and other non-religious people were included in the study to understand their own religious and cultural perspectives on the issue at hand - mental illness in West Africa. The inclusion of different religious groups or faith-based individuals will be so helpful in a future study on mental illness, and to understand similarities or differences in spiritual perception of mental illness. Another group of participants in the survey was doctors or mental health workers who practiced or worked in West Africa. They were able to narrate their experiences of interacting with a mentally ill person in West Africa. The health care professionals will also be able to explain some issues they encountered in treating those with mental illness.

The Participants considered for inclusion in the interview were family members or friends of someone that had a mentally ill person in West Africa because they would be able to narrate the scope of stigma and social distancing on both the mentally ill and their families in West Africa. The family member of a mentally sick individual will also be in the position to explain societal reactions to the diagnosis and treatment of mental illness by a health care professional in West Africa. The inclusion of a family member of a mentally ill person as one of the participants in the study helped us to understand the type of treatment they utilized in the initial onset of diagnosis of mental illness to a family member.

Participant Exclusion Criteria

The people excluded in the selection criteria were those below the age of 18. The people below 18 years are minors, and they may not be exposed to mental illness perceptions and stereotypes in West Africa before they migrated to the United States. Also, excluded in the interview process were those with suicidal thoughts or hallucinations. People with suicidal thoughts or hallucinating may not have correct information about mental illness in West Africa. Also, those excluded from participating in the study were persons that expressed their dissatisfaction with the research or those who were uncomfortable discussing mental disease due to trauma experienced in the past about it or those it could trigger out counter transference talking about it. Also, excluded to participate in the study were those with dementia or end of life issues, which could prevent them from remembering the past.

Recruitment of Participants from West Africa

The first step utilized in my recruitment of participants for the study was to contact potential participants through phone calls and later emails to notify them of the proposal. The number of participants approached for the review was initially 32, but out of the 18 people who responded, each had extra 8 others for our consideration and analysis, as noted in our abstract, and they freely showed their willingness to participate in the study. Those people who did not respond to our request gave excuses that they were busy with their jobs, or they were out of town. Some participants for the interview were referrals from other people from West Africa that knew they could contribute immensely to the study of mental illness perceptions in West Africa. Other participants in the study came through a religious group of West Africans residing in Philadelphia.

Out of the 32 people that accepted to participate in the interview, fourteen people were not allowed to participate in the interview process. Two of those excluded in the interview process reported that they came to the United States when they were young and had no thorough knowledge about mental illness in West Africa, and the other people stated that they were not well educated to express themselves and discuss mental illness perception in West Africa. The remaining 18 main participants in the study were screened and included in the interview process. The 18 participants and their collaborators for the study were each given 7 to 14 weeks' notice to prepare for the physical face-to-face interview. They selected individual participants for the study and were also sent a letter in writing informing them about the topic, the date, the time and place to meet for the in-depth interview. The time for the interview meeting was between 45 minutes to 60 minutes, and the selected participants were informed. The participants' replies for accepting the schedule came through phone calls, text, or email messages.

The initial date, time, and place of the interview was acceptable to 13 of the 18 selected participants, while the other five participants gave a new schedule of the time and place that was acceptable to both the interviewer and participants. A letter of consent was typed and prepared for each of the participants to sign on the date of the meeting. The participants were each given a copy of the interview questions and how to answer each question. The participants were told to ask questions if they have any matter of concern to discuss before the interview proceeded. Surprisingly, the interview proper, for the different participants lasted for more than two months.

The total participants in the interview process were 18 people (12 men and six women) whose ages ranged from 30 to 75 years, including the other 8 participants being actively enrolled by the initial participants. The participants in the study included 4 Nigerians; 2 Ghanaians; 2 Sierra Leoneans; 3 Liberians; 2 Burkina Faso; 1 Malian; 1 Togolese; 1 Ivory Coast; 1 Guinea; 1 Benin Republic. A total of 10 countries from West Africa participated in the study. The composition of the participants included 2 Pastors; 1 Catholic Priests; 3 Health Care Professionals; 3 Caregivers; 2 Teachers; 2 Older Adults; 2 Leaders of a group in the Church; 2 Business Men; 1 Social Worker plus the eye-witness accounts of the co-opted members.

The 11 questions for the in-depth interview were typed out, validated and given to each participant on the date of the interview, and the questions were asked in sequence to get the best answers from participants. The participants were also asked to elaborate on the issues as much as they could on each of the questions. The signed consent form was collected from each of the participants before the interview commenced, and the participants got assurance that their names would be kept confidential.

A snowball recruitment method was utilized to get other potential participants from West Africa to participate in the study as some communities are smaller in number in Philadelphia (Alvarez, Vasquez, Mayorga, Fester & Mitrani, 2006). In addition to the 11 questions utilized in the interview, a Mental Illness Stigma Scale (MISS) was given to each of the participants to rate the level of stigma against the mentally ill persons in their own culture in West Africa (Day, Edgren & Eshleman, 2007). The Likert scale on the scale of 1- 7 (denoting disagree entirely, to agree ultimately) was given to the participants to rate their perception of mental illness in West Africa.

Focused Group Recruitment

The initial people invited for the focus group discussion were ten people from West Africa. The invitation to participate in the focus group was done through phone calls and later emailed to potential participants informing them of the study on "Cultural Perceptions of Mental Illness": Perceptive of West Africans in Philadelphia." Out of the ten people invited, eight (80%) accepted the invitation. The eight participants that agreed to participate in the study were informed more than 5 weeks earlier through email of the study place, date, and time. The focus group participants were also reminded twice about the study through phone calls and emails before the date of the survey.

The eight participants invited for the group discussion were informed that the time for the study would be between 30 minutes to one hour, and the topic for the study was communicated to each potential participant in the group. The questions for the group discussion were sent to each participant to prepare in advance for the conference. The study participants were each chosen from different countries in West Africa comprising as noted already: Nigeria, Ghana, Togo, Benin Republic, Burkina Faso, Liberia, and Sierra Leon, et cetera. The educational level of the participants ranged from high school to master's level degree, and their professions included three home caregivers, one nurse, one social worker, and two business people. The age of the group participants ranged from 35 to 60, and they all lived in West Africa for many years before migrating to the United States.

On the date of the focus group study, 7 out of the eight invited people came for the study. The participants got informed that "respectfulness" should be accorded to each participant in the focus group and that participants should avoid criticism or optional argument, but instead, use it as a time to learn from each other. A consent form was given to each of the 7 participants to sign before they started the discussion. The participants were informed about taking a turn in answering the study questions based on their cultural perception of mental illness.

Ethical Issues

There was a consideration of ethical issues in this study of "cultural perception of mental illness" in West Africa. The participants utilized in this study were assured of their safety; no harm either emotionally, physically, mentally, socially, and psychologically before the commencement of the study interview. There was elaborate information to participants on the topic of discussion before participants signed the consent form to participate in the study. The participants were also asked to participate voluntarily without pressure.

The criteria utilized for the research focuses on three Belmont principles on ethical issues - respect for persons; beneficence, and the burden and benefit principle. Respect for a person's belief was communicated and observed so that participation in the research study was voluntary, and participants were respected irrespective of their social and cultural background. The beneficence principle of no harm is to increase the participant's willingness to participate in the research. It was the reason that the names of study participants were anonymous – never unmentioned, but instead their initial was used in the study. The burden and benefit principle was to be made known to participants during and after to inform participants about the survey of mental illness perception in West Africa. The study participants were also guaranteed confidentiality with the signing of the confidentiality form, that readers will not identify their answers on the cultural perception of mental illness in West Africa.

Participants Responses

Participant 1: (Nigeria).

The first participant interviewed said that there were stigmas associated with mental illness in Nigeria by the use of names like "crazy dogs." The mentally ill persons in Nigeria are sometimes not allowed to stay with healthy people. The participant thought that mental illness was transferable, and people should avoid marrying from a family of anyone that has a mental illness. The participant also said that people avoid the "mentally ill people because they are filthy, dirty, and smelling." The participant maintained that mental illness was comparable to diseases such as depression, diabetes, and cancer, which in the western world may be in the family gene; the same belief applies to mental illness in Nigeria. The participant acknowledged the idea that mental illness was caused by "curses," "evil spirit attack", or medical issues. The participant also said that

Nigerians believe in the diabolical power of an evil person to curse an average normal person to be mentally ill. The participant also noted that some ordinary people use mentally sick persons to beg for money or work in their farms with no pay. The participant stated that lack of education, poverty, and proper treatment centers were the reasons the mentally ill persons were uncured. The participant also said that mentally ill persons are not shown love or compassion, as they are chained, not fed, and called different bad names.

Participant 2: (Nigeria):

The second participant also said that Nigerians believe that mental illness is caused by curses or curses from the ancestors. The participant said that it is a shame to have a mentally ill person in the family because of the stigma associated with it. The participant reported that lack of love is the reason the sick mentally person responds in anger. They are chained and left in the rain and sun with no caring for them. It is this lack of love that makes the mentally ill persons aggressive against some people, but not against those that care for them. There is a saying in Nigeria "that the family of the mentally ill person feels the shame and not the mentally ill person" *(Ihere anaghi eme onye ara, kama, obu ndi ezi na ulo ya ka ihere na-eme).* It is this shame that makes families of some mentally ill persons to reject and distance themselves from accepting their member with mental illness. What a devastating and demoralizing effect on the mentally-ill person! It is the stigma and fear of transmission that makes people avoid marrying from a family of one diagnosed with mental illness. The second participant also agreed that there is a fear among Nigerians that the mentally ill persons are dangerous and can overpower others, and this is the reason they are chained. Some mentally ill persons are used by their captors to beg for alms in the street. This participant stated that the government is responsible for the problem of mental illness in Nigeria because of a lack of treatment centers and education on mental illness.

Participant 3: (Nigeria)

The third participant in my interview process stated that the mentally ill persons are chained to prevent escape from their family. Sometimes, the mentally ill persons are chained and beaten with a cane as a way of casting out the devil responsible for the mental illness. The participant also agreed that "curses," "evil spirits", and "spell" are the major causes of mental illness. He said that there is a notion that the mentally ill person is dangerous and can harm others. The participant reported that the people of Nigeria do not marry from families where there is a mental illness, to prevent mental illness from being transferred to the next generation.

Participant 4: (Burkina Faso):

The participant reported that there are lots of mentally ill persons in Burkina Faso, and most of them live at their parents' houses, while about 30% to 40% do not have a home, and wander about in the street. The participant maintained that some of the mentally ill people that live outside of their homes have nobody to take care of them, and they include children or adults. The participant said that the cause of the mental illness is evil spirit possession, ancestral curses, and drugs. The participant maintained that psychological reasons like maltreatment by others and magical curses placed on a person could cause mental illness. The participant also reported that drug abuse could equally lead to mental illness.

Remarkably, the participant recommended that people should treat the mentally ill person like human beings by listening to them and providing for their feeding and clothing. The participant noted that mentally ill persons are accepted sometimes at the initial time but later rejected due to financial constraints and being dangerous, due to the same reason. As there is an English saying that "a hungry person is an angry one". The participant also said that some people use spiritual treatment or traditional herbs for mental illness treatment.

Participant 5: (Burkina Faso):

The participant said that the mentally ill persons are the sick who live in the street with nobody to take care of them. The participant noted that mentally ill people eat whatever they can get from roaming around the streets in search of food and through begging. The sick mentally persons often do not remember things, may not have clothes to wear, neither take their shower nor maintain cleanness.

The participant also said that mental illness is caused by witchcraft or by other mysterious ways and by demons. The participant said that disobedience to cultural beliefs, sickness, and social issues might lead to mental illness. The inability of people to go for medical checkup or diagnoses may lead to mental illness. The mentally ill person may be accepted in the family but refused to stay in the same house with other families if the mentally ill persons are presumed to be unpredictable as to harm others.

The participant said that people call the mentally ill persons "mad," "foolish", and children are often afraid to see them. The participant narrated the story of a doctor who is mentally ill in their town and lived in the street, but can prescribe medication for people who ask him. The participant said that mental illness treatment in Burkina Faso is through biogenic medicines, prayers, and traditional medicine. The participant said that he could allow those with mild mental health diagnoses to live with him but not those with major mental illness issues. The participant equally noted that the greatest need for those with mental illness is to be taken care of by both the family and the government. The participant noted that the conditions of those with mental illness are, most often, pitiable in West Africa, and they need care to prevent them from being in the street.

Participant 6: (Ivory Coast)

The participant said that brain malfunction, stress, and depression could cause mental illness. Another cause as reported by the participant is through curses, spell, and not going for medical examination. The participant said that when a mentally ill person goes to the hospital for testing and nothing is found, it points to curses or evil spirit possession, and in that case, prayer is the preferred method of treatment. The prayers for the mentally ill persons possessed by evil spirits are often conducted by an exorcist priest who had the gift of healing and deliverance to cast out the devil. The participant maintained that the mentally ill people whose sickness is not caused by evil spirit possession could use traditional herbs for treatment.

The participant said that self, family, or spell cast by others the affected person has offended may cause mental illness. The participant noted that in Ivory Coast, the mentally ill persons are sometimes picked up in the street and taken to mental hospitals for treatment. The participant said that the best form of treatment is through prayer, biogenic, and traditional healing. The participant said that the government should establish a firm policy on mental health treatment to prevent mentally ill people from going to the street. The participant maintained that the mentally ill persons should be valued and treated well by providing them with food, shelter, and proper treatment.

Participant 7: (Liberia)

The participant reported that mentally ill people are mad and people thought that mental sickness is caused by witchcraft. The participant said that some mental illnesses are caused by war due to depression or frustration as was the case in Liberia. The participant reported that some people joined the Liberia civil war after losing all their properties, and ended up with mental illness. Drug use was another cause of mental illness in Liberia, and people consulting with fetish priests who asked them to keep certain rituals and that failing to follow those rituals may result in mental illness. Some people got mental disease due to jealousy by wicked people who used charms or witchcraft on them.

The participant also observed that women are the ones that suffer most from depression due to economic hardship, sicknesses, and are abandonment by the husband, and loss of a family member during the civil war. The participant equally underlined that mentally ill persons are not accepted because they are assumed to be dangerous. The problem with mental illness in Liberia is that there is no rehabilitation center available to take care of the mentally sick, and those living in the street are abandoned. The stereotypes against the mentally ill in Liberia include – calling them mad people, crazy, and unimportant people in the society. The participant maintained that due to economic reasons and lack of mental health hospitals, most mentally ill persons patronize the witch doctors and traditional herbalists for treatment. The participant's perception is that they can live with the mentally ill if they know when the mentally ill person is about to have a crisis, and how to control it at that moment. The participant also said that they could not live with a mentally ill person if it is not possible to manage them during a crisis.

The participant said that the problem with traditional healers is that they do not know the correct dosage of the herb they are giving their clients, and it might cause more harm than healing the mentally ill person. The traditional healer also does not know the chemical reaction of whatever prescription they are giving the mentally ill person, and if the prescribed herbs did not work, they might use a cane to beat the sick mentally person until he or she calms down. The participant reported that they are not feeling happy seeing a known person with mental illness because the person is supposed to be contributing to society. The participant said that the best way to care for the mentally ill people is to show them kindness, caring, talking, or counseling them. The participant also noted that the mentally ill could only harm people if they are not shown love and are made to be angry. The best way to get along with the mentally ill person is to talk to them gently and ask them to do chores and take a shower, but do not force them to do things. The use of rehabilitation centers is necessary to accommodate the mentally ill persons, especially those in the street.

Participant 8: (Togo).

The participant reported that the cause of mental illness in Togo is demons, deformity from birth, and curses from other people. The participant maintained that mental illness, like some other sicknesses, is transferable. According to the participant, mental illness is not many in Togo due to the natural food eaten in their country. The participant maintained that the rate of drug use in Togo is meager due to the people's culture of avoiding synthetic foods and drinks. The participant perception is that their people's belief in God is preventing the rampant cases of mental illness, as seen in other cultures in West Africa. There is also a belief in Togo that the mentally ill persons are dangerous and can harm others.

The participant said that poverty is another cause of mental illness, especially when people cannot afford a daily meal, and eventually, it results in depression. The best way to tackle mental illness is to accept them in society and create treatment centers where they can receive treatment. It is a lack of treatment centers that generate more problems for the mentally ill, as they end up going to quacks where the problem gets worse. The participant also said that biogenic medication or traditional medicine could be utilized to cure mental illness, but the healing of mental illness caused by a demonic attack is through deliverance prayers.

Participant 9: (Nigeria).

The participant said that the carelessness of the sick person causes mental illness by not taking care of himself or going for a routine medical check-up. It is the result of this carelessness in making one's health relevant that leads to some of the mentally ill being in the street or dying early, and not always witchcraft as they thought might be. The participant contended that it is better to educate the people on the importance of exercise, eating good food, and avoiding artificial foods or drinks that may lead to sicknesses. The participant said that when people are not taking care of themselves, diseases might come, which may lead to depression or another type of mental illness. The participant noted that most people from West Africa work every time without resting the brain activities and it can lead to mental illness too.

The participant reported that the mentally ill are accepted in their culture if they are not harmful to others. The people also believe that when sick mentally people yell, it is a sign that they see a "spirit", and some can start running away or start doing strange things unconsciously. The best way to curtail mental illness according to the participant is to see the doctor most often for a check-up and to use local herbs to calm those already diagnosed with mental illness. The participant said that the problem with traditional healing in West Africa is that conventional healers either overprescribe or under prescribe the medication, and it prevents the cure of mental illness sickness.

The participant maintained that he could live with a mentally ill person to help him do certain things like showering and to assist in providing him food. It is also good to redirect the mental person positively to achieve other items for self. The participant said that people should not treat the mentally ill persons bad, like chasing them away or yelling at them as it might create more signs of hatred for them. The participant contended that people should treat the mentally ill person as he or she wants others to manage them, and people study them and ask questions on what they want to do or need.

Participant 10: (Ghana)

The participant said that people get mental illness through the use of drugs or are born with it. The participant also reported that some mental illnesses came through a spiritual attack, family curses, or curse by someone the mentally ill person has offended. The participant maintained that the mentally ill persons in West Africa have the right to live and should not be ignored or abandoned. Though, some people in Ghana see the mentally ill person as stupid who should not live or work with others to avoid harm. The participant reported that people in Ghana view the mentally ill as dangerous who can harm another person anytime or throw things to others without any reason.

The participant maintained that the government should provide rehabilitation centers to care for those with mental illness rather than leaving them at the mercy of God. The participant said that the mentally ill should be taken to the psychiatrist as soon as it is noticed to avoid degenerating into a severe situation. The participant also noted that the local herbs are used sometimes, but it should be monitored to prevent over-prescription of herbal medicine. The participant said that deliverance prayer should be used to cure those whose mental illnesses are associated with the demonic attack. The participant also noted that the provision of the necessities of life like food, clothing, and shelter would help to reduce mental illness in West Africa.

Participant 11: (Liberia).

The participant said that people perceive mental illness as witchcraft in Liberia. He mentioned that demons or witchcrafts possess even a child diagnosed with mental illness. There is no age difference in the negative perception of mental illness as caused by witchcraft, so the treatment method is mostly the traditional herbs. The participant reported that if a mentally ill person goes out naked in the street, it means that mental sickness is incurable. The perception by the participant is that the mentally ill persons are aggressive, and that is the reason they are chained, and called all sorts of abusive names.

The participant maintained that drug use and any sickness that can affect the brain like seizure could cause mental illness. The perception among most people is that mental illness came through witchcraft attacks or other forms of demonic manipulation. The participant narrated that if traditional medicine does not work, the mentally ill are allowed to roam the street in search of help. The participant from Liberia does not view those with depression or anxiety as mentally sick but seen as miserable individuals. The participant contended that he could live with mild mental illness individuals, but not with those with severe mental illness.

The participant said that the governments in West Africa are not doing enough to assist individuals with mental illness by providing mental health institutions to treat them as to reduce the burden incurred by families in caring for their mentally ill members. The participant suggested the importance of making proper diagnoses before the treatment of mentally ill persons. The importance of providing food, shelter, and clothing, and even jobs for the mentally sick by the government is necessary to improve their wellbeing. The participant pinpointed the importance of education in West Africa to curb the mentality that mental illness is all about witchcraft.

Participant 12: (Liberia)

The participant said that drugs and alcohol use is the leading cause of mental illness in Liberia. She also said that poverty, stress, and demonic attacks could cause mental illness. The participant maintained that "demonic orientation" like consulting an evil person for riches and taking an oath can lead to mental illness if the persons fail to abide by the pledge. The participant said that people think that mental illness is caused mostly by witchcraft, and so they are called "crazy." The participant reported that mentally ill persons are not cared for or receive any benefit from the government.

The mentally ill persons are untreated in West Africa with proper drugs, and people may make a mockery of them. Some people from West Africa do not see mental illness as sickness, but something funny. The participant said that people should advocate on behalf of the mentally ill persons. The importance of education is necessary according to the participant to curb the negative stereotypes against the mentally ill individual. In this instance, laziness is a form of mental illness. The participant said that some people do not believe that prayer alone can cure a mentally sick person. The participant, however, recommended that deliverance is still essential especially those mental illnesses perceived to be caused by witchcraft. The participant also suggested that people should support the government by contributing to the building of psychiatric hospitals and counseling centers.

Participant 13: (Mali)

The participant reported that the perception is that the mentally ill people are nobody in their culture. They may wander from one place to another with no purpose. The mentally ill persons are seen as those that act funny, confused, and without future. The participant believes that mental illness is caused by witchcraft, but might be caused by other factors. The participant maintained that some mentally ill family members take them to the traditional herbalist for treatment due to lack of psychiatric hospitals. The participant also said that the conventional healer might compound the problem by giving the mentally ill person herbs that are dangerous and untested. The participant said that their people do not believe that western medication can cure mental illness.

The participant said that the mentally ill people are thought to be dangerous, crazy, and they can harm another person, so they are not allowed to live with other people. The participant suggests that the government can open mental illness treatment centers or psychiatric hospitals to care for the mentally sick individuals. The government should also take away the mentally ill persons roaming in the streets and provide them with shelter, treatment, and food.

Participant 14: (Sierra Leon)

The participant said that the mentally ill persons do not reason usually. They are vulnerable, and both the government and society do not care about them. The notion among most people in West Africa is that a demonic attack causes mental illness, and any child with mental illness is thought to be a snake. The participant reported that people make fun of the mentally ill persons and nobody likes to keep them in their house. The report is that people may ask the mentally ill person to dance for them in public, and cane might be used to flog the mentally ill person, and non-disabled men may rape some. The mentally ill may also be physically abused and given hard labor to do as to provide them with a plate of food. The family members of a mentally ill person may be ashamed to acknowledge knowing their own person with mental illness, and the family members may also distance themselves from them. The participant said that due to the mentally ill being uncared for, they might escape to go out to look for food in the trash bags or beg from outsiders. Most of those with mental illness in West Africa are treated as an outcast and caricatured by other people.

The participant said that some mental illness in their country is caused by the use of drugs, especially among the youths. Another cause of mental illness is the lack of jobs, which results in drug use by teens. The participant maintained that some mentally ill persons are born with it, while some mental illness comes as a result of membership in an occult group. The secret member that fails to perform their assigned rituals may end up being mad or having a mental illness. Some of the stereotypes against mental illnesses are that it is untreatable because of the demon in the mentally ill person. The participant suggested that the best way to prevent mental illness is to create jobs in West African countries, control drug sales, and use, establish treatment centers for mental illness treatment, and provide food, shelter, and clothing for the mentally ill persons.

Participant 15: (Benin Republic)

The participant reported that diseases, curses and toxic drugs cause mental illness and it affects the brain. The participant also said that voodoo or witchcraft manipulation causes mental illnesses. The participant maintained that people from their country prefer to use traditional medicine due to shortage or unavailability of biogenic medications to treat mental illness. The mentally ill persons often feel that people will kill them, so they get scared and want to run away from their families. The participant said that the mentally ill persons may not remember things or where they are at a given moment, and it is the reason they roam about the street from one place to another and sleep anywhere they find. The participant said that people are scared to live with the mentally ill because of the notion that they are dangerous and can harm a person.

The participant said that the lack of government policy on mental illness is hindering its treatment in West Africa. The participant acknowledged that education is essential to decrease the stigma and negative perception of mental illness in West Africa.

Participant: 16 (Sierra Leon)

The participant said that mental illness as was the case in Sierra Leon was caused by war because people lost their homes, properties, and loved ones during the war. It is the loss of people, properties, and valuables that caused depression and other forms of mental illness. The participant also reported that the governments in most West African countries do not care about the mentally ill people, so they are abandoned to their families who may not have resources to take care of them. The families of the mentally ill person may not want to see them because of the fear that they are dangerous and can harm others.

The participant maintained that due to the abandonment of the mentally ill to their fate, most of them go out from their families to look for food on trash bags. The families of mentally ill persons that are financially buoyant provide for them or keep them at centers where they are taken care of by others. The participant said that the government in Sierra Leon tried a bit to assist the mentally ill by keeping them out of the streets, but the war caused their abandonment and subsequent increase of the mentally ill in their country. The participant said that the government in West Africa should provide necessary resources like schools, mental hospitals, and counseling centers to care for the mentally ill people.

Participant: 17 (Ghana)

The participant said that curses against a person and depression from sickness cause mental illness. The participant also reported that the most significant cause of the mental illness is lack of education caused by not going for medical checkup and ignorance in seeking proper medical treatment in West Africa. The participant said that lack of resources and family support sometimes causes people to develop mental illness. The mentally ill are also seen as worthless in society and do not deserve support from the community. The mentally sick left outside are abused physically by other healthy people.

The participant said that the treatment of mental illness is by herbs which in some cases are not effective in West Africa. The participant noted that some people are also born with mental illness, and most people in West Africa do not know other forms of mental illness except psychosis. The participant reported that the governments in West Africa are not doing enough to help those with mental illness. The participant said she can live with a mentally ill person if she can redirect them. The participant suggested that people should know that the mentally ill people in West Africa are human beings in need of care, and the government should provide facilities for their treatment. The participant also said that education is essential to bring awareness of the dangers of stigmatization against mentally ill persons in West Africa.

Participant 18: (Guinea)

The participant said that mental illness could come through congenital disability or by the use of drugs in West Africa. Also, mental illness can come through curses or the wickedness of someone against another. The participant also said that poverty is another cause of mental illness in West Africa. The participant reported that people avoid mentally ill persons because they are dangerous and can hurt someone. The participant maintained that the mentally ill in West Africa have lost their senses and behave in strange ways. The mentally sick, most often, pick their food from the trash bags, and they can sleep on the streets or bushes.

The participant verbalized that the dangerously mentally ill persons can kill if they are provoked by people, so that fear makes people avoid them. The mentally ill in West Africa are mostly treated with local herbs by traditional healers, and sometimes the medication makes them more dangerous because of the side effects of the drug. The participant said that some mentally ill are chained to prevent their escape, and makes them more dangerous as their freedom is compromised. The participant also said that governments in West Africa are not helping the mentally ill in the area of providing food, shelter, and proper treatment, so it makes them wander from one place to another.

Table 2: Participants' Demographic Information

Participants Initial	Age	Country of Origin	Profession	Gender
BN	35	Nigeria	Priest	Male
CO	55	Nigeria	Doctor	Male
EB	53	Ghana	Caregiver	Female
EM	48	Sierra Leon	Health Care	Female
MA	75	Nigeria	Older Adult	Male
SA	58	Ghana	Nurse	Female
HC	54	Burkina Faso	Caregiver	Male
PF	58	Mali	Caregiver	Female
LM	45	Togo	Business Man	Male
MJ	65	Sierra Leon	Older Adult	Female
FA	46	Ivory Coast	Church Leader	Male
OB	50	Guinea	Business Man	Male
SK	70	Benin Republic	Older Adult	Male
EH	46	Liberia	Church Leader	Female
LD	56	Burkina Faso	Health Care	Male
TS	52	Liberia	Health Care	Male
GO	62	Nigeria	Pastor	Male
PS	66	Liberia	Health care	Female

Table 3: Participants' Social Demographic Variables

Participants Initial	Age	Participants yearly income	Marital Status	Education
BN	35	N/A	Priest	MA
CO	55	85,000	Married	Doctor
EB	53	40,000	Married	BA
EM	48	48,000	Single	BA
MA	75	16,000 (welfare)	Widower	High School
SA	58	65,000	Married	Nurse
HC	54	28,000	Married	High School
PF	58	25,000	Unmarried	High School
LM	45	50,000	Single	High School
MJ	65	18,000 (welfare)	Married	Middle School
FA	46	36,000	Married	BA
OB	50	42,000	Married	BA
SK	70	14,000 (welfare)	Married	High School
EH	46	30,000	Divorced	High School
LD	56	24,000	Married	High School
TS	52	38,000	Divorced	BA
GO	62	52,000	Married	MA
PS	66	45,000	Married	BA

Table 4: Number of Participants' Answers to Data Questions

Data Question	Participants Response	Number of Respondents to the question.
Q. 1	Mental illness is untreatable disease	12 out of 18
Q. 2	Mental illness is caused by demons and curses.	15
	Mental illness is caused by individual and parents sin.	13
	Mental illness is caused by drugs	8

	Mental illness is caused by evil spirit, curses and drugs	16
Q.3	Mentally ill people are crazy and stupid	12
	Mentally ill persons are dirty and dangerous	16
Q.4	Mentally ill are acceptable in West African Culture.	4
	Mentally ill people are not acceptable in West African culture	16
Q.5	Mentally ill people are dirty and unpredictable.	14
	Mentally ill people are socially avoided in West Africa.	13
Q.6	West African People prefer traditional method of treating mental illness	6
	People from West Africa prefer spiritual/ religious method of mental illness treatment	7
	Both the traditional and spiritual are preferred method of mental illness treatment.	10
Q.7	They will not accept a mentally ill person to live or work with them.	13
	They can live with a mentally ill person.	3
	They are not sure if they can live with a mentally ill person	2
Q.8	Mental illness is not well diagnosed or treated in West Africa.	12
	Governments in West Africa are not doing enough to help the mentally ill people	15
Q.9	They feel bad seeing a person the know has mental illness	18
Q.10	Mental illness can be treated best with biogenic medication.	5
Q.11	Mental illness is incurable and affects both the individual and the family.	14

Table 5: Participant's Demography Of Religious Affiliation

PARTICIPANTS COUNTRY OF ORIGIN	RELIGIOUS AFFILIATION
1. NIGERIA	CHRISTIAN
2. NIGERIA	CHRISTIAN
3. GHANA	CHRISTIAN
4. SIERRA LEONE	MUSLIM
5. NIGERIA	CHRISTIAN
6. GHANA	CHRISTIAN
7. BURKINA FASO	CHRISTIAN
8. MALI	MUSLIM
9. TOGO	CHRISTIAN
10. SIERRA LEONE	CHRISTIAN
11. IVORY COAST	CHRISTIAN
12. GUINEE	MUSLIM
13. BENIN REPUBLIC	CHRISTIAN
14. LIBERIA	CHRISTIAN
15. BURKINA FASO	CHRISTIAN
16. LIBERIA	MUSLIM
17. NIGERIA	CHRISTIAN
18. LIBERIA	MUSLIM

CHAPTER FOUR

DATA ANALYSIS

—ᘛᘚ—

Evidence of Mental Illness Perception and Stigmatization in West Africa from Literature Reviews

Using the literature reviews to analyze West African people's perception on mental illness, points to the belief that mental illness is caused by "evil spirits" (Achiga, 2016; Yendork, Kpobi & Sarfo, 2016), and as a curse from God (Stefanivoics, et al., 2016; Kpobi &Swartz, 2018) or by spiritual, physical problems, curses, and spell (Monteiro & Balogun, (2014). Another literature review article reported mental illness as a diabolical interference in the life of a person (Onyina, 2002) or that mental illness is associated with demon possession (Asamoah, Osafo & Agyapong, 2014; Ae-Ngibise et al., (2010)). The result from some literature review studies acknowledged that substance abuse, evil spirit possession, hereditary, traumatic events, shock, spells, or God's curse on a person causes mental illness (Achiga, (2016; Makanjuola et al., 2016). There is also the perception in the literature review that mental illness is infectious and should be avoided to prevent others from being infected (Achiga, (2016).

The literature reviews also pointed out that stigmatization is a problem among those with mental illness in West Africa and it reduces the mentally ill person from whole to one with low social rank and devalues them in the society (Gyanfi, Hegadoren & Park, 2018). Data from the literature review also pointed out that mental illness stigmatization comes through social distancing (Bello-Awusah, Adedokun, Dogra & Omigbodun, 2014), and the mentally ill persons are dangerous, crazy and unpredictable (Mfoafo-M'Carthy, Sottie & Gyan, 2016). There is also stigmatization of the mentally ill persons through alienation, stereotype, and social withdrawal (Brohan et al., 2011).

The literature reviews' articles on mental illness in West Africa reported that the mentally ill persons are discriminated against by family members, the community, and even health care workers (Brohan et al., 2011). The denial of the mentally ill persons from getting a job, education, and health care makes them live a life of fear, guilt, isolation, and segregation (Gyanfi, Hegadoren & Park, 2018). The family members of those diagnosed with mental illness in West Africa are, sometimes, discriminated against by others in marriage (Kadri et al., 2004; Gureje et al., 2005). The stigmatization of the mentally ill person also manifests in the form of reduced societal networks and devalued self-esteem (Gaebel et al., 2011). The literature reviews reported that other forms of stigmatization and ill-treatment against the mentally ill persons come through molestation, flogging, denial of education, insults and forceful introduction to early marriage (Aremeyaw, 2013; Asamoah, Osafo & Agyapong, 2014) and that the best way to dispel rumors and stigmatization on mental illness in West Africa is mainly through education (Achiga, 2016).

Data Evidence from Participants Interviewed

The data from participants interviewed among West Africans showed that 16 (89%) out of the 18 people interviewed say that evil spirits, curses, demons, and drugs are responsible for mental illness, and it confirms the findings from the literature reviews that a demon, evil spirit, and curses cause mental illness (Achiga, (2016; Makanjuola et al., 2016; Yendork, Kpobi & Sarfo, 2016; Asamoah, Osafo & Agyapong, 2014; Ae-Ngibise et al., 2010).

Also, 12 (67%) of the 18 interviewed participants believe that mentally ill persons are crazy and stupid, while 16 (89%) out of the 18 study participants view mentally sick persons as dirty and dangerous. It confirms the perception of West Africans in the literature reviewed articles that mentally ill persons are dangerous and unpredictable (Mfoafo-M'Carthy, Sottie & Gyan, 2016). The majority of the study participants (16 out of 18) 89% said that the traditional and spiritual treatment methods are more effective and preferred among West Africans to treat mental illness.

The notion among West Africans is that since demons and evil spirits cause mental illness, the western biogenic medication may only serve to suppress symptoms of mental illness for a short time, so the traditional methods of using herbs and prayers of exorcism help in the cure of mental illness. All the participants (100%) in the study acknowledged that the government policy on mental illness in West African countries is not suitable for mental illness diagnosis and treatment. The participants maintained that most West African countries do not care about the mentally ill persons or support in their welfare. The study participants also said that lack of education is responsible for the lack of diagnosis and treatment of the mentally ill persons in West Africa. This finding confirms with the literature reviewed articles that lack of knowledge is responsible for the negative stereotypes and stigmatization against the mentally ill persons in West Africa (Achiga, 2016; Gyanfi, Hegadoren & Park, 2018).

Focus Group – Analysis of Mental Illness and Stigma Perception in West Africa

The research questions, the Likert scale, and the Mental illness Stigmatization Scale were used to understand the focused group participants' views on mental illness perception in West Africa. Out of the 7 participants that participated in the group interview, 5 (71%) acknowledged that witchcraft, curses, and drugs cause mental illness. Two of the participants (29%) reported that lack of medical check-up and depression is the cause of mental illness.

On the issue of hereditary, 5 participants (71%) agreed that mental illness is transferrable, and individuals would not like to marry from a family of someone with mental illness. Two of the participants (29%), however, do not agree that that mental illness is transferable. All 7 group participants (100%) expressed negative views of government policy on mental illness in West Africa. Four out of the seven participants (57%) acknowledged that the best treatment for mental illness is through traditional medicine, and two of the participant (29%) said that prayer or deliverance is the best method of curing the mentally ill persons. One participant (14%) in the focus group, however, noted that biogenic medication is the best form of mental illness treatment. However, 6 out of the 7 participants (86%) verbalized that the combination of traditional medicine and deliverance would be their best bet in the treatment of mental illness in West Africa.

All the participants acknowledged that lack of education is the primary reason for the stereotype and myths against the mentally ill persons in West Africa. Also, 4 participants (57%) reported that they would not accept to live with mentally ill persons because they are dangerous and unpredictable, but two participants (29%) said that they would agree to live with a mentally ill person if their mental illness is mild or moderate. One participant (14%) said that he could live with a mentally ill person if he knows how to control the mental illness during a crisis.

Focus Group Result Analysis Using the Likert Scale

A total of 7 participants participated in the focus group by using the Likert Scale to understand the cultural perception of mental illness in West Africa. Out of the seven participants (n=7) interviewed in the focus group, 5 participants agreed that there is a high level of stigma against the mentally ill in West Africa, which represents 71% of the total participants. Also, 5 out of the 7 participants in the group are of the view that witchcraft, curses, or drugs cause mental illness. A total of 4 participants maintained that the best treatment for mental illness is with traditional medicine, which represents 57% of the total number of participants. The whole 7 participants (n=7) agreed that government policy is not favorable on mental illness treatment. As it were, all the 7 participants decided that lack of education is a significant hindrance to mental illness prevention in West Africa, and 4 (57%) out of the 7 participants view mentally ill persons as dangerous and unpredictable.

Likert Scale Result from Participants used in the Interview Process

(Likert Scale is a scaling system where respondents are asked to rate items on a level of agreement – strongly agree, simply agree or disagree, etc.). Thus, a total of 18 participants, plus their co-opted, were interviewed by using the Likert scale, and the result showed that all the 18 participants (n=18) agreed that mentally ill persons are stigmatized against in West Africa by others, which represent 100% acceptance of stigmatization. Also, 17 out of the 18

(94%) participants either strongly agree or merely agree that mental illness is caused by "demon," or "evil spirit's" manipulation. A total number of 12 (67%) participants agree or strongly agree that mental illness is best treated by using traditional medicine, while another 14 (78%) participants disagree or strongly disagree that the government in West Africa policy on mental health is favorable. A total number of 9 participants (50%) said that they could live or work with mentally ill persons, while 14 participants agree or strongly agree (78%) that mental illness is transferable.

Data from Participants Interviewed using Mental Illness Stigmatization Scale (MISS)

The result from the 18 participants that participated in the interview shows that mentally ill persons in West Africa are stigmatized or discriminated in the area of housing (78%), education (78%), finding a job (56%), social life 14 out of 18 participants (78%), mental health workers 10 out of 18 participants (56%) and avoidance 15 out of 18 participants (83%).

Triangulation

Triangulation is a research observation of using two or more methods in a qualitative study to validate the result of a study (Flick, Kardorff & Steirike (2004). The triangulation of data is also a way to approach data verification from different perspectives and interviews or survey to validate the authenticity of a study. In triangulation, data can be gathered from various sources or people to assess the utility and trustworthiness of a study (Flick, Kardorff & Steirike (2004).

In the study of the "Cultural Perception of Mental illness" in West Africa, triangulation was used to understand the relationship or connection between findings in the literature reviews and data from personal interviews of participants on their perceptions of mental illness in West Africa, as to find the validity or the authenticity of the study. The use of triangulation is a good step in the analysis of different findings of the survey of cultural perception of mental illness among West African immigrants in Philadelphia.

The data used in the triangulation of mental illness perception in West Africa are from the literature reviews utilized in the study, individual participant's interviews and a focus group, the Likert Survey, and Mental Illness Stigmatization Scale (MISS). The essence of using these data was to find the commonality or differences of perceptions using the triangulation tool. The data from the literature reviews, participant's interviews and Likert scale using the triangulation methods showed that people from West Africa believed that demons, curses or evil spirit cause mental illness (Achiga, (2016; Makanjuola et al., 2016; Yendork, Kpobi & Sarfo, 2016; Asamoah, Osafo & Agyapong, 2014; Ae-Ngibise et al., 2010).

The triangulation of the literature reviews, participant interviews, and Likert scale points to the common belief among West Africans that mentally ill persons are dangerous and unpredictable. The triangulation of the study shows that people from West Africa acknowledged that the use of traditional medicine and exorcism, prayer are the favored way of mental illness treatment. The triangulation of the study also shows that most people from West Africa are blaming the government policy on mental illness as the cause of poor mental illness diagnosis and treatment in West Africa. The common belief is that governments in West Africa are uncaring in the provision of mental health hospitals, diagnostic and counseling centers to assist in mental illness treatment.

The use of triangulation of the literature reviews, participant interviews, Likert and mental illness stigmatization scales also shows that lack of education is a hindrance to mental illness treatment in West Africa. The general belief is that most people of West Africa are ignorant of the etiology of mental illness or go for a medical check-up or seek proper diagnoses when they are sick. Some participants used in the interview process hinted that lack of "love" is what is responsible for the stigmatization, stereotypes, and negative perception of mental illness in West Africa. The participants maintained that it is the lack of love that is responsible for not providing medical care, shelter, clothing, and food to the mentally ill persons in West Africa. The use of triangulation in the study of cultural perception of mental illness among West Africans in Philadelphia helped to reduce biases in the research.

Credibility

Credibility is when readers find inferences in the interpretive research to be believable. The reliability of interpretive research is maintained through accurate transcription of interviews, correct records during data collection and analysis, and it is when readers find inferences in the interpretive research to be believable. It is through accurate transcription of interviews, correct records during data collection, and analysis that the reliability of interpretive research is maintained.

The use of credibility in qualitative research is to outline the rigor or integrity of the study on the cultural perception of mental illness in West Africa. The reliability of this study on mental illness perception in West Africa will also help readers to appreciate methods and soundness of the study, and to understand the standard by which research can be judged (Noble & Smith, 2015).

The credibility and transferability of qualitative design can be enhanced when the researcher provides evidence that the current environment for the study works in another setting. To enhance reliability and transferability, the researcher must also demonstrate that the findings are from the data and not personal ideas. In creating a research design, the researcher must be sure that the accurate picture is scrutinized and presented with the research method used. The use of triangulation can help to validate the credibility of data utilized in a study. Triangulation of the source, the process, and with other researchers will help to confirm the reliability and transferability of research from the audit trail.

The credibility of research depends on the believability and trustworthiness of the findings, and when readers find inferences in the interpretive research to be believable. The reliability of interpretive research is maintained through accurate transcription of interviews, correct records during data collection and analysis. The use of triangulation can be used to verify the accuracy of data provided by participants. It is essential for participants to understand that the findings are accurate and credible. The credibility of research is valid when the researcher presents the real picture of the phenomenon under investigation, and future researchers can arrive at the same conclusion, and the result could be the same in a different environment.

The coding process was used to identify similar themes and ideas on this study on the cultural perception of mental illness by West Africans. It helped to identify patterns, such as keywords, phrases, ideas, and themes that are used frequently in the study. To define, classify the code and label of this research study, the existing theories from literature reviews and new ideas from interview data and prior systems were used to understand mental illness perception among West Africans. The research questions and responses from participants were useful to identify a priori codes on this dissertation topic on "Cultural Perception of Mental Illness" by West Africans in Philadelphia. Constant comparing of systems from texts on the subject of study was useful to ensure consistency in the work. After getting the codes, it was sorted into groups and sub-groups such as types or kinds. It is the categorizing of the systems into what they represent that forms the bases for the data analysis.

The credibility of this study on "Cultural Perception of Mental Illness" in West Africa shows similarity on the causes, stereotypes, and perceptions of mental illness among West Africans. Reports from the literature review articles and data from individual interviews, the focus group, the Likert scale, and mental illness stigmatization scale survey points to the same cultural perception of mental illness in West Africa, and it attests to the credibility of this study.

Documents Analysis as a Qualitative Research Method

Document analysis is an important research method that can strengthen the knowledge-based and understanding of qualitative research. It is exciting because it was previously viewed as a document and not a research method. The essence of document analysis has its advantage in reducing biases and increasing credibility. It supports the need for planning on what type of issue a researcher wants to investigate and the type of questions the researcher wants to ask participants during interviews and surveys.

The area of designing is necessary to find out the way forward in a research project. Designing helps to understand what kind of participants, resources, and timeline is suitable for qualitative research. This topic is essential because it shows the need to start early in planning, designing, and doing this research project on "Cultural Perceptions on Mental Illness" in West Africa. It helps in planning the type of questions to ask participants during the interview process as noted already.

The document analysis was used to identify the useful articles to utilize in the literature review portion of this study on the cultural perception of mental illness in West Africa. The need to use relevant articles on mental illness in West Africa is critical and helped to support data collection done through interviews and observations. The opinion is that document analysis helps to know the strength and weaknesses of articles used in research or dissertation, but it has not been mentioned often or used effectively. Proper understanding of document analysis will guide researchers into obtaining evident-based facts of a proposed dissertation topic like the "cultural perception of mental illness in West Africa."

Another advantage of document analysis is that it works best in conjunction with other qualitative methods such as interviewing and observations as a means of triangulation. It is through triangulation that researchers will evaluate the quality of their research. The use of documents analysis in this dissertation topic on mental illness perception in West Africa helped to explore the cultural beliefs of West Africans on mental illness and **triangulate** (or shape the various sides or angles of the items in order to find out how they relate) the observation during the interview process. The document analyses are ways to get good literature review articles and it helped to get good articles that discussed mental illness perception in West Africa.

Content Analysis

The contents in literature reviews and data gathering of this study on "cultural perception of mental illness" in West Africa were used to code information gathered in the study. Coding is the process of organizing data into themes, ideas, and categories for further analysis. The coding method used helped to make a comparison between the literature reviews, data from interviews, Likert scale survey, and Mental illness Stigmatization Scale (MISS) as to identify cultural perceptions of mental illness in West Africa. The coding pattern in this study used common themes, terms, phrases, and keywords identified in the study of cultural perception of mental illness in West Africa. The process of determining the coding involves a thorough reading of the literature reviews and data gathered from interviews and surveys of those that participated in the study to identify patterns and keywords of interest.

The first thing done in the study was to identify similar wordings from the literature reviews on the causes, the perceptions, stereotypes, and treatment methods of treating mental illness in West Africa. The related words that occur in the literature reviews were called Priori codes. The information gathered from participants interviewed in the study and identified the same causes of mental illness as the literature review articles were also classified as Priori codes. The ideas or opinions in the literature reviews and interviews that were different from the commonly identified causes of mental illness in West Africa are called the "emergent codes." Constant comparison of data from the literature reviews and participant's interviews were made to know the differences and similarities in the data set.

In coding, this study on mental illness perception in West Africa, a color of "red" code was used to identify West Africans perceptions of the causes of mental illness as – infection, curses, evil spirit, poverty, lack of education, lack of diagnosis and treatment facilities, drugs, trauma or wars, parents' sin and punishment from God. The "yellow" color code was used to identify stereotypes against the mentally ill persons in West Africa, and it includes – stigmatization, avoidance, name-calling (mad, idiot, crazy, useless, dangerous), and not marrying from a family of one with mental illness. The "blue" color code was used to identify perceived treatment or prevention of mental illness in West Africa like education, training of mental health workers, building mental health hospitals, diagnostic centers and counseling places, good government policy, provision of jobs and provision of essential amenities (food, clothing, and shelter) to mentally ill persons and prayer or deliverance.

Thematic Analysis

The thematic analysis is commonly used to analyze data in a qualitative research study, and it helps to pinpoint patterns or themes in the study of "cultural perception of mental illness" in West Africa. According to Braun and Clark (2006), thematic analysis helps in identifying, analyzing, and reporting patterns.

The thematic analysis allows for the use of the multicultural theoretical framework of understanding different cultural perceptions of mental illness from people of West Africa. It allowed for a detailed description of data obtained from participants in the study. The thematic analysis also allows pinpointing common themes or patterns from the literature reviews article and interview data that have standard meanings or relationships (Braun & Clark, 2006). The thematic analysis helped to pinpoint common perception among West Africans that mental illness is caused by "evil spirit, curses, drugs, poverty, spells, and God's punishment. It also shows the stereotypes identified in both the literature reviews and interview data as – avoidance, name-calling (crazy, idiot, mad, useless), not marrying a mentally ill family member, job denial, and eviction from homes.

Coding Method

APriori Codes from my Literature Reviews:

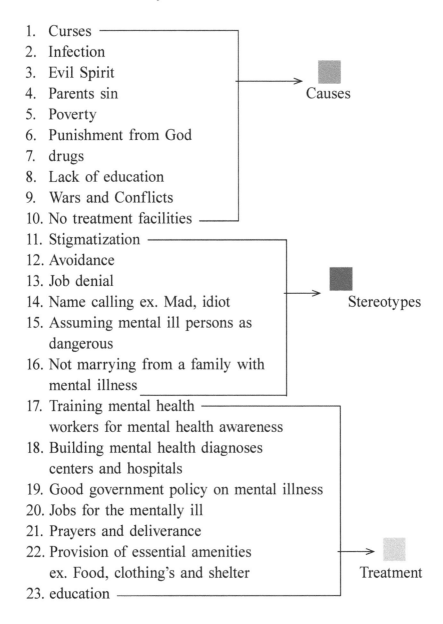

1. Curses
2. Infection
3. Evil Spirit
4. Parents sin
5. Poverty
6. Punishment from God
7. drugs
8. Lack of education
9. Wars and Conflicts
10. No treatment facilities

Causes

11. Stigmatization
12. Avoidance
13. Job denial
14. Name calling ex. Mad, idiot
15. Assuming mental ill persons as dangerous
16. Not marrying from a family with mental illness

Stereotypes

17. Training mental health workers for mental health awareness
18. Building mental health diagnoses centers and hospitals
19. Good government policy on mental illness
20. Jobs for the mentally ill
21. Prayers and deliverance
22. Provision of essential amenities ex. Food, clothing's and shelter
23. education

Treatment

Emergent Codes from my Data analysis

1. "People do not like to marry from families of mental ill persons due to fears of inheritance" – **stigmatization;**

2. "Mental ill persons are flogged as means of treatment or chained on a tree to prevent them from escaping" – **stigmatization;**

3. "Mental ill persons are starved and not loved, so they tend to be aggressive sometimes" - **No love;**

4. West African people believe that mental illness can be caused due to parent's sin or nemesis or curses" - **Curses, sin;**

5. "People believe that it is a shame to have mental illness in a family" – **Stigmatization;**

6. Poverty in West Africa causes mental illness – **Cause;**

7. War and stress in West Africa can cause mental illness – **Causes;**

Data from literature Reviews

1. Most West African people believe that mental illness is caused by evil spirits or witchcraft (Achiga, 2016) - **witchcraft, evil spirit;**

2. Some health care professionals believe that mental illness is caused by evil spirit possession, spell or curse by God and it results in stigmatization (Achiga, 2016) - **Evil spirit, curses or spell;**

3. Some West African people believe that the mentally ill persons are dangerous and can harm themselves or others (Achiga, 2016) – **dangerous;**

4. Beliefs have resulted in stigmatization of those with mental illness (Stefanovics, et al., 2016) – **Stigmatization;**

5. People portray mentally ill persons as "mad", "idiots" (Mfoafo-M'Carthy, 2016) – **stigmatization;**

6. Unawareness and lack of treatment facilities are other causes of mental illness and it makes the mentally ill persons to seek treatment at the herbalist place (James et al., 2016) - **Hindrances to treatment;**

7. Training church members and community health workers can help prevent mental illness (Iheanacho, et al., 2015) - **Prevention strategies.**

Table 6: Mental Illness Stigmatization Scale (MISS) Result from Participants Interview

Questions	Not at all	A little	Moderate	A lot
1. Have the mentally ill person been treated unfairly in making friend or keeping friends?	0	1	4	13
2. Have the mentally ill been treated unfairly by people in your neighborhood?	0	1	2	15
3. Have the mentally ill been treated unfairly in dating or intimate relationships?	0	2	3	13

4. Have the mentally ill been treated unfairly in housing?	0	3	3	12
5. Have the mentally ill been treated unfairly in education?	0	1	3	14
6. Have the mentally ill been treated unfairly in marriage or divorce?	0	0	1	17
7. Have the mentally ill been treated unfairly by your family?	0	3	6	10
8. Have the mentally ill been treated unfairly in finding a job?	0	4	4	10
9. Have the mentally ill been treated unfairly in keeping a job?	0	5	5	8
10. Have the mentally ill been treated unfairly when using public transport?	2	4	5	7
11. Have the mentally ill been treated unfairly in getting welfare benefits or disability pensions?	1	3	5	9
12. Have the mentally ill been treated unfairly in your religious practices?	1	3	6	8
13. Have mentally ill been treated unfairly in their social life?	0	2	2	14
14. Have the mentally ill been treated unfairly by the police?	2	3	6	7

15. Have the mentally ill been treated unfairly when getting help for physical health problems?	1	3	5	9
16. Have the mentally ill been treated unfairly by mental health staff?	1	3	4	10

Questions	Not at all	A little	Moderate
17. Have the mentally ill been treated unfairly in levels of privacy?	1	2	4
18. Have the mentally ill been treated unfairly in their personal safety and security?	0	1	2
19. Have the mentally ill been treated unfairly in starting a family or having children?	0	2	4
20. Have the mentally ill been treated unfairly in roles as a parent to children?	0	2	2
21. Have the mentally ill been avoided or shunned by people who know that they have a mental health problem?	0	1	2
22. Have the mentally ill been treated unfairly in any other areas of life?	2	3	4
23. Have the mentally ill been stopped from applying for work?	6	3	4

24. Have the mentally ill been stopped from applying for education or training courses?	7	2	3
25. Have the mentally ill been stopped from having a close personal relationship?	5	2	4
26. Have the mentally ill been concealed or hidden their mental health problem from others?	0	2	4
27. Have the mentally ill made friends with people who don't use mental health services?	1	3	5
28. Have the mentally ill been able to use personal skills or abilities in coping with stigma and discrimination?	0	0	3
29. Have the mentally ill been treated more positively by their family?	0	1	2
30. Have the mentally ill been treated more positively in getting welfare benefits or disability pensions?	13	3	1
31. Have the mentally ill been treated more positively in housing?	12	1	3
32. Have the mentally ill been treated more positively in religious activities?	2	3	4

Table 7: Likert Scale Participants Analysis Result

Questions	Strongly Disagree	Disagree	Agree	Strongly Agree
1. Mental illness is caused by demonic or evil spirit attack	0	1	3	14
2. Mental illness is better treated by using traditional medicine.	2	2	6	6
3. Mental health policy in West Africa is favorable	14	2	6	6
4. Mentally ill person in West Africa can live or work with you	5	4	4	5
5. Mental illness is transferable or hereditary:	1	3	5	9

Table 8: Result with Percentage from Interviewed Participants

Cultural Perception of Mental Illness in West Africa	Respondents out of 18 + the copted Participants	Percentage of Respondents (%)
Mental illness is untreatable	6	4
Mental illness is caused by demons and curse.	8	5.6
Mental illness is caused by individual or parents sin.	6	4
Mental illness is caused by drugs.	4	2.8
Mental illness is caused by evil spirit, curses and drugs.	9	6
Mentally ill people are crazy and stupid.	6	4
Mentally ill persons are dirty and dangerous.	9	6

Mental illness is acceptable in West Africa.	4	2.8
Mental illness is not acceptable in West Africa.	10	7
Mentally ill person is dirty and unpredictable.	7	5
Mentally ill persons are socially avoided in West Africa	6	4
Traditional method is preferred to treat mental illness.	5	3.5
Spiritual method is preferred to heal mental illness.	5	3.5
Traditional and spiritual is best to treat mental illness.	6	4
Will not live or work with a mentally ill person.	6	4
Will live or work with a mentally ill person.	2	1.5*
Not sure if they will live or work with a mentally ill person	2	1.5*
Mental illness is not well diagnosed or treated in West Africa.	6	4
Government policy is not good on mental illness in West Africa.	8	5.7
Not happy seeing a familiar person with mental illness.	15	10.7
Biogenic medication is best treatment for mental illness.	3	2
Mental illness is incurable and affects individuals and family.	7	5
Total	**140**	**100%**

N/B: *Remember that as observed in our abstract, out of our 18 participants, each of them co-opted 8 other participants in our search, which brought the total to 144, but after the researcher's redistribution and validation of the data collected, 4 numbers dropped out of the 144, bringing the reliability index to 140.*

Table 9: Result with Percentage from Focus Group Participants Using the Research Questionnaire:

Cultural Perception of Mental Illness:	Number of Respondents Out of the 7+11 Participants	Percentage of Respondents (%)
Mental illness is caused by witchcraft, curses or drugs.	15	10.7
Lack of diagnosis is responsible for mental illness.	4	2.8
Mental illness is hereditary and can be transferred.	15	10.7
Have negative views of government policy on mental illness in West Africa.	4	2.8
Mental illness is not transferrable	14	10
Mental illness is best treated with traditional medicine.	10	7
Mental illness is best treated through prayers.	8	5.7
Mental illness is best treated through biogenic medication.	10	7
Combination of traditional medicine and prayer is best for mental illness treatment.	15	10.7
Lack of education is responsible for mental illness stigma.	14	10
Mentally ill persons are dangerous and unpredictable.	11	7.8
Can live or work with a mentally ill person.	4	2.8
Cannot live or work with a mentally ill person.	8	5.7

Not sure if can live or work with a mentally ill person.	8	5.7
Total	140	100%

Table 10: Mental Illness Stigmatization Scale Result from some of the Focused Group:

Research Questions	Number of Participants	Respondents Positive Answers (Yes)	Respondents Negative Answer (No)
Mental illness caused by witchcraft, curses and drugs.	7	5 (71%)	2 (29%)
Mental illness is transferable	7	5 (71%)	2 (29%)
Government policy is not good for mental illness in West Africa.	7	7 (100%).	0 (0%)
Mental illness is best cured by traditional medicine.	7	4 (57%)	3 (43%)
Mental illness cured by traditional medicine and prayer	7	6 (86%).	1 (14%)
Lack of education is responsible for stigma against mental illness	7	7 (100%)	0 (0%)
Will accept to live or work with a mentally ill person	7	3 (43%)	4 (57%)

CHAPTER FIVE

RESULTS SUMMARY

It has to be noted that 18 participants (n=18) plus the 8 being co-opted, bringing the total number of participants to 140 in the interview process to understand the cultural perception of mental illness in West Africa. A focus group of 7 participants (n=7) also participated in an interview to understand the cultural understanding of mental illness in West Africa. A Likert scale and Mental Illness Stigmatization Scale (MISS) were also utilized to survey participant's perception of mental illness in West Africa.

The study shows that the negative perception of mental illness in West Africa originated from the ancestors of people of West Africa who believed that mental illness was non-treatable, transferable and a sign of bad omen to the family and the belief has continued to the present generation. It is the cynical belief on mental illness that has continued to generate stigmatization against individuals diagnosed with mental illness. One of the first types of stigma in West Africa against the mentally ill identified in the study is avoidance. The perceived result from participants in this study is that the mentally ill person is dangerous and can attack another person at any time. The participants also agreed that there is perceived avoidance against the mentally ill and it comes in the form of social restraint, deprivation of needs like clean clothes, housing, and healthful foods. The result of the study also showed that it is the stigma against the mentally ill that leads to the poor treatment of the mentally ill by mental health professionals.

The study noted that the common belief on mental illness among immigrants from West Africa is that mental illness is not treatable but associated with curses, demon possession, or witchcraft (Stefanovic et al., 2016; Achiga, 2016)). The result from the study shows that the negative perceptions on mental illness are responsible for the lack of diagnoses and treatment of those with mental illness in West African (Stefanovics et al., 2016). The negative perceptions have also led to mental illness stigmatization and brutality against mentally ill individuals in West Africa ((Gyanfi, Hegadoren & Park. 2018; Gureje et al., 2005).

Another result identified in the study of mental illness in West Africa is that the governments of countries in West Africa have not taken proper notice to understand that mental illness is not a taboo, but treatable disease. The result of the study shows that ignorance by the governments in West Africa is responsible for their failure to invest financially in the diagnosis and treatment of mentally ill persons. The study observed that government policy on mental health is not well established in most countries in West Africa, and the majority of countries in West Africa have no mental health centers or hospitals to refer the mentally sick for counseling, diagnoses, and treatment. The result of the study also identified not only the lack of mental health centers but also the lack of trained mental health personals or professionals as the hindrance to the proper treatment of the mentally ill persons (Walker, 2015).

The result of the study on mental illness from the literature review and participants data gathered through the interview process point out on common perceptions among West African that mental illness is caused by "evil spirits" (Achiga, 2016; Yendork, Kpobi &

Sarfo, 2016), and as a curse from God (Stefanivoics, et al., 2016; Kpobi &Swartz, 2018) or by spiritual, physical problems, curses, and spell (Monteiro & Balogun, (2014). The result of the study also reported that mental illness is a diabolical interference in the life of a person (Onyina, 2002) or that mental illness is associated with demon possession (Asamoah, Osafo & Agyapong, 2014; Ae-Ngibise et al., (2010)). The result of the study from the literature review studies and individual data from interviews also reported that substance abuse, evil spirit possession, hereditary, traumatic events, shock, spells or God's curse on a person also caused the mental illness (Achiga, (2016; Makanjuola et al., 2016). The study result points to the common perception among West Africans that mental illness is infectious and should be avoided to prevent others from being infected (Achiga, (2016).

Both the literature reviews and participants data's on the study also pointed out that stigmatization is a problem among those with mental illness in West Africa, and it reduces the mentally ill person from being whole to one with low social rank and devalues them in the society (Gyanfi, Hegadoren & Park, 2018). The result of the data also points to the basic fact the mental illness stigmatization in West Africa comes through social distancing (Bello-Awusah, Adedokun, Dogra & Omigbodun, 2014), and that mentally ill persons are dangerous, crazy and unpredictable (Mfoafo-M'Carthy, Sottie & Gyan, 2016). The study result also said that the stigmatization of the mentally ill persons is through alienation, stereotype, and social withdrawal (Brohan et al., 2011). The study result noted that persons diagnosed with mental illness are sometimes chained together and asked to go about in the town begging money for their captures. The study identified that the inhumane treatment of those with mentally ill might lead to untimely death because of starvation and flogging with a cane. The result of the survey also shows that the mentally ill persons in West Africa are untreated because they are assumed to be unpredictable and can attack another person at any time.

The result of the study on mental illness perception in West Africa noted that sometimes the mentally ill persons are kept in the open day and night and chained on a tree to prevent their escape. The mentally sick persons chained on a tree are beaten by rain, sun, and bugs, and are left on the same spot both in the day and at night. The result shows that the food deprivation against the mentally ill persons in West Africa may lead them to escape from their family as to go out and search for food in trash bags, and they end up consuming foods that are contamination or disease-infested– which may lead to their untimely death. The study reported that the mentally ill person who goes around begging for decent food from people in the community are most often chased away with a stick or beaten with rod or stick. The result of the study also shows that the mentally ill in West Africa often go about without clothing, and they wander around the environment naked, and they may have wounds all over their body that are caused by infections.

The study noted that there is stigmatization against the mentally sick persons and their families through avoidance by relatives, friends, and the society (Gureje et al., 2005; Gyanfi et al., 2018). The study points out that the stigma associated with mental illness in West Africa often leads to avoidance from other people to marry from families of a mentally ill person (Kadri et al., 2004). There is the perception that mental illness is inheritable, and marrying from the family of a mentally ill will be transferred to the other family (Kadri et al., 2004).

The study contended that there is a non-recognition of mental illness as sickness in West Africa and improper treatment of mental illness is caused by poverty. The result from the study acknowledged that in West Africa countries, mental illness is most prevalent in rural areas where also the rate of poverty is very high (Eaton et al., 2017). It is the poverty coupled with the negative perception that makes the mentally sick person not to seek a solution to cure of the mental sickness (Lund et al., 2013). The result of the study also shows that mentally ill persons live the life of fear, guilt, isolation, and segregation because of their denial in getting jobs, education and health care (Gyanfi, Hegadoren & Park, 2018) and it make them live a life of fear, guilt, isolation, and segregation.

The result of the study acknowledges that the significant cause of the negative perception of mental illness in West Africa is the lack of education (Achiga, 2016). The study maintained that lack of schooling poses the greatest hindrance to mental illness understanding, diagnoses, and treatment (Gyanfi et al., 2018). The study points out that it is the combination of lack of knowledge, poverty, and lack of mental health facilities that are responsible for hindering mental illness treatment in West Africa (Gyanfi et al., 2018). The result of the study shows that economic hardship among most families in West Africa makes the mentally ill persons seek treatment with quacks or traditional healers who do not know about mental illness treatment (Eaton et al., 2017; Agyapong et al., 2015). The study identified from the literature reviews and participant data reported that the native doctors use incantations, herbs, and sometimes flogging to cast out the presumed demons on the mentally sick as a way of mental illness treatment (Asuni, 1990). The result of the study also shows that traditional healers who use herbs are untrained on the dosage and effects of the medicine prescribed to the mentally sick person, and it may compound their illness (Asuni, 1990).

The result of the study on mental illness perception in West Africa acknowledged that education about mental illness by counselors and clinicians would help to create awareness on mental health types, causes, and diagnosis, and treatment methods. The result also maintained that education would help to dispel rumors that mental illness is inheritable, untreatable, or associated with a demon. The study agreed that with proper knowledge and provision of good mental health centers, the problem of stigmatization against the mentally ill person in West Africa would decrease (Kabir et al., 2004; Yendork, Kpobi & Sarfo, 2016). The study maintained that counselors and clinicians' advocacy for mentally ill persons in West Africa would help them to have subsidized cost in mental illness treatment. The result of the study encourages counselors and clinicians to advocate that the mentally ill persons be shown 'love' through the provision of good food, housing, and proper treatment.

The result of the study maintained that communities recognize the traditional practice of healing as one of the best methods of treating mental illness in West Africa (Kpobi, Swartz, Omenyo, 2018), and the conventional healers engage in community recognized methods of healing which is peculiar to their communities in West Africa as to achieve wellness (Kpobi, Swartz, Omenyo, 2018; Onyina, 2002; Asamoah, Gyadu, 2013). The study also reported that the traditional healers are utilized more for healing in West Africa due to their cultural beliefs and values, and it forms part of their health-seeking behavior (Kpobi, Swartz, Omenyo, 2018). The result equally showed that traditional healers provide holistic care that involves the social, cultural, and emotional needs of people from West African peoples due to proper cultural understanding of their mental illness (Kpobi, Swartz, Omenyo, 2018).

The study noted that West Africans believe that mental sickness has to do with emotional or psychological natures and are a punishment from gods for evil, so western medicine is helpless towards the cure within this context. Also, people from West Africa see western medicine as what gives temporary relief to mental illness remedy, and it accounts for the preference of mental illness treatment with local herbs and indigenous drugs.

There is a belief among West Africans that mental illness cure could be through prayer and deliverance because of the notion that mental illness is caused by "evil spirit attack", "curses" and "God's punishment." The result of the study points out that with the emergent of new Pentecostalism in churches, the demon responsible for mental illness will be cast out through prayers. The current belief in Pentecostal and Charismatic healing has helped to form the health-seeking behavior of those with mental illness to try prayers of deliverance to heal the mentally ill person. The result also shows that the mentally ill who profess spiritually healed might be asked to testify before the public that they were cured through prayers and it continues to draw more followers who believe in the efficacy of prayers to cure mental illness.

The result of the study identified why the study of mental illness is essential – to create awareness about the mental illness myths, stereotypes, to decrease stigmatization, for workforce harvest and economic growth, and to dispel rumors associated with mental illness in West Africa. The study also observed that family members of a mentally ill person sometimes find it challenging to take a mentally ill individual in their family for treatment to prevent the portrayal that a mad person is in their family.

Conclusion

Summarizing this section, we need to observe that there is a cultural perception in West Africa that demons, unclean spirits, drugs, witches, and God's punishment cause mental illness. The negative understanding of mental illness has led to non-diagnoses and treatment of those with mental illness in West Africa. The governments in West Africa have not been at the forefront to confront the challenges of mental illness that have led many mentally ill persons to death through the same neglect due primarily to a lack of proper diagnoses and treatment to save lives.

This study implicated the obvious fact that creating awareness would help in proper diagnoses and treatment of the mentally ill persons. The problem with those diagnosed with mental illness in West Africa is that they do not seek the services of a health professional for treatment or they do not have mental health facilities to consult or they lack financial resources to care for themselves. It is the lack of these services that makes the mentally ill persons seek treatment with quacks or herbalists who are unaware of the side effects of what they prescribe to their clients.

The health care professionals, clinicians, and counselors should be trained on cultural awareness, respect for cultures and to know the myths of mental illness in West Africa before proceeding to treat those diagnosed with mental illness (CMHS, 1998). The governments in West Africa should have a grass-root policy on mental illness that would focus on mental health diagnoses, treatment, and delivery (Eaton et al., 2017). The need for proper education starting from school children to adults is vital to decrease myths and discrimination against the mentally ill persons. There is also a call to use churches, mosques, and hospital staff to dispel rumors that mental illness is untreatable, infectious, and caused by demon possession (Iheanacho et al., 2015). The government in West Africa should be involved in teaching or educating its people from same West Africa about other treatments that could be used to cure mental illness, like medication and psychotherapy (Ae-Ngibise et al., 2010).

The monitoring and inclusion of traditional medicine men into a central body by the governments in West Africa will be useful to curtail abuses and be suitable for the production and disbursement of evidence-based conventional medicine for mental illness treatment. The involvement of communities and families is reiterated as essential to dispel the negative rumors on mental illness perception in West Africa. The pastoral counselors should advocate and educate people from West Africa on how to eradicate stigma against the mentally ill persons in West Africa.

The study concluded that there is a need for more research to understand the impact of culture on mental illness and its effect on people from West Africa, and how it is impacting misdiagnoses and mistreatment of mental illness. A person's knowledge of mental illness in West Africa is that it goes with a psychotic disorder, so psycho-education is necessary to teach mentally ill persons' how to manage the crisis, like during depression mood, anxiety, psychosis, and panic attacks (Yendork et al., 2016). The use of education for mental illness treatment is also essential for West Africans to identify different treatment options and approaches.

This study will help psychotherapists to use their skills in psychotherapies that are culturally adaptable to treat people from West Africa suffering from mental illness. According to Potocky-Tripodi (2002), most people from West Africa diagnosed with mental illness are afraid to go for therapy due to cultural, family, and social influences that would portray them as "mad" (Mfoafo-M'Carthy, 2016). So, this study will inform mental health practitioners how cultural awareness that includes - respect for the culture, the tradition, and beliefs of West Africans are essential in the therapeutic process (CMHS, 1998). The study will help counselors working with West Africans to understand the differences or similarities in mental health understanding, diagnosis, and treatment between the Western World and people from West Africa.

This study on mental illness perceptions and stigmatization will be vital for the governments of West Africa to establish a new policy on proper diagnosis, treatment, and mental health delivery. It will also help the governments in West Africa to develop a grass-roots policy that will include education and adequate training for mental health personals (Eaton et al., 2017). The grass root policy by the governments in West Africa will also help to establish mental health institutions where proper diagnosis, treatment, and adequate medicines for mental illness treatment will be disbursed (Iheanacho et al., 2015). It will help the governments in West Africa to establish mental health centers in rural areas, where there are usually more persons with mental illness. The study will enlighten West Africans to understand other methods that will be useful to treat mental illness and create awareness of the truth about mental illness. The use of churches, mosques, schools, and other worship centers will also be useful to dispel the negative rumors on mental illness (Iheanacho et al., 2015). It will help governments, society and individuals to understand other methods of treating mental illness, like psychotherapy, and embrace other modern means of mental health treatment (Ae-Ngibise et al., 2010).

This study on mental illness perspective in West Africa will help West African governments to integrate the traditional medicine healers into one body as to curtail abuses in mental illness treatment, and to ascertain the benefits of the conventional medicine. The inclusion of local medicine healers will help to improve the standard of production of the local medication, its prescription, and disbursement to the mentally ill persons (Ae-Ngibise et al., 2010). The government may be asked to partake in sponsoring the production of evidence-based traditional medicine for mental illness treatment.

There is another major contribution to understanding mental illness perception in West Africa, precisely the involvement of communities in dispelling rumors on the culturally perceived myths about mental illness that it comes through divine punishment, hereditary, spiritual attack, drug, and magic (Kabir et al., 2004). This study will help to bring to awareness that some cultural norms about mental illness are unacceptably feasible with modern civilization.

This research on mental illness perception and stigmatization will help pastoral counselors to understand the culture and spirituality of people of West Africa, and the therapeutic process to use in counseling individuals, groups, and communities affected by mental illness stigmatization. It will also educate pastoral counselors on the diverse cultures of people from West Africa, such as social norms, religious rites, and other cultural norms that cause stigmatization of the mentally ill persons. Understanding the problem associated with stigmatization will help to educate pastoral counselors to know their own biases and values, especially in working with people from West Africa. Awareness of mental illness stigmatization will also help pastoral counselors to seek justice in communities of West Africa where there are injustices.

Education is the most crucial counseling tool to decrease stigmatization (Kabir et al., 2004), so educating pastoral counselors on methods to eradicate stereotypes and negative perceptions on mental illness will lead to the use of appropriate intervention strategies to reduce stigmatization against the mentally ill persons in West Africa. Proper education by pastoral counselors and other mental health professionals will help to understand the mental process of communities in West Africa and how to proceed in counseling the people. It will also help to know if there are other physical or environmental factors responsible for the stigmatization of the mentally ill persons. The study will help people of West Africa to understand the causes of mental illness and to learn new skills to decrease stigmatization against the mentally ill persons (Stefanovics et al., 2016).

The study of mental illness perception and stigmatization among West Africans will lead to more research on the impact of culture on mental illness to avoid misdiagnoses and improper treatment. This article on mental health perception and stigmatization will help to examine how self-identity and beliefs contribute to mental illness perception among West African, and the frame of reference for mental illness treatment. The study will discuss how family dynamic and social integration and community involvement can help in fostering the healing of mentally ill persons from West Africa.

Further Discussions

The study highlights some of the issues that come with stigmatization against the mentally ill persons, like denial of basic amenities, social distancing by others, and physical, psychological, social, and sexual abuse against the mentally ill persons in West Africa. The negative perception of mental illness in West Africa starts from childhood to adulthood and manifests in the form of social distancing (Oduguwa, Adedokun & Omigbodun, 2007). The study maintained that what the mentally ill people experience is all negative in their interaction with families, communities, and society. The mentally ill are also stigmatized by family members, and it can be through rejection, food denial, and chaining on a tree where they are beaten by rain and sun, or through social distancing, physical, social, psychological, and sexual abuses. The issue of discrimination does not end with society only but includes discrimination from health care workers. The health care professionals who stigmatize the mentally ill include the psychiatrists, psychiatric nurses, social workers, and mental health workers. Thus, they must be cautious as professionals!

The negative perception of mental illness is in line with the notion that mentally ill persons are unpredictable, dangerous, dirty, and can attack other people with or without provocation. It is also the attitude of some mental health workers that makes it difficult for the mentally ill persons to get proper care in health care settings. The stigma against the mentally ill includes **the denial of adequate education and employmen**t. The study maintained that the mentally ill persons experience guilt because of the way they are looked down upon in the society and how they cannot apply for a job; seek education and training (Gyamfi, Hegadoren & Park, 2018). The issue of stigma against the mental illness in West Africa can make the mentally ill person not to seek treatment, and may cause the mental sickness to become chronic (Gur et al., 2012). The study reported that mentally ill persons are sometimes not given the necessary medication or care needed by the patient for recovery. It is the lack of knowledge about mental illness that often leads to mood instability, increased hospitalization, and decreased psychosocial functioning (Ritsher & Phelan, 2004). The chaining of mentally ill persons is to checkmate lousy behavior and prevent escape in West Africa (Read, Adibokan & Nyame, 2009).

The study discussed that stigmatization against families of a mentally ill person also comes through avoidance by relatives, friends, and the society (Gureje et al., 2005; Gyanfi et al., 2018). The stigma associated with mental illness in West Africa often leads to avoidance from other people to marry from families of a mentally ill person (Kadri et al., 2004). The study discussed the perception in West Africa that mental illness is inheritable, and marrying from the family of a mentally ill person can be transferred to another family (Kadri et al., 2004). The stigma against the mentally ill persons also comes in the area of job denial and accessibility to quality health care. The study discussed the need for a proper understanding of mental illness causes, diagnosis, and treatment to decrease stigma against the mentally ill person. The stigma against the mentally ill is also perceived to lead to the loss of self-esteem and self-efficacy (Watson et al., 2007).

Lack of education is the greatest hindrance to mental illness treatment in West Africa. The discussion maintained that education about mental illness should start from the grass-root level, starting from schools, churches, mosques, health care centers, and hospitals to create awareness on the truth about mental illness (Gaebal et al.,

2011). Mental illness awareness can also be done through campaigns, billboards, and seminars to decrease the negative perceptions of mental illness in West Africa. The study discussed that it is a lack of knowledge that is responsible for the bad choices of treatment for mental illness in West Africa (Yendork et al., 2016). Some families of a mentally ill person patronize traditional healers who are unaware of the side effects or dosage they prescribe to their clients.

The cause of mental illness as perceived by West Africans includes – low income (Lund et al., 2013), lack of housing, marital and financial problems (Owitti et al., 2015, substance abuse (Kabir, Iliyasu, Abubakar & Aliyu, 2004). The study discussed that mental distresses, like intense anger, worry, guilt, stress, bereavement, and grief, can lead to mental illness (Owitti et al., 2015). Other social factors, like lack of housing, financial difficulties, marital problems, and interpersonal issues may lead to mental illness, lack of education, poverty, and unemployment are cited also as the primary cause of mental illness in Ghana (Osei et al., 2012). There is a perception that chronic poverty and unstable environment can lead to mental illness (Pigeon-Gagne et al., (2017). The study discussed that other mental health challenges experienced by most West African countries are linked to civil wars and unemployment as was the case in Liberia and other West African countries ravaged by war (Atindanbile & Thomson, 2011). The study identified other causes mentioned as responsible for mental illness in West Africa like alcohol and drug use, divine punishment, evil spirit, and trauma (Kabir, Iliyasu, Abubakar & Aliyu, 2004), and symptoms may manifest through aggression, talkativeness, acentric behavior, and wondering.

The discussion is that psycho-cultural belief, religion or spiritual beliefs, social difficulty, cognitive impairment, disaster, economic hardship, and substance abuse cause mental illness in West Africa (Monteiro & Balogun, 2014). Mentally ill patients with psychosis can show unusual behavior or have significant depression and anxiety that manifest through negative emotions, and they are mostly considered to have a mental illness (Monteiro & Balogun, 2014).

The study includes other factors apart from the culture that shapes the use of traditional healing (Ae-Ngibise et al., 2010), and these include economy and social factors, the inadequacy of mental health staff, resources, insufficient medications in developing countries (Ofori-Atta, A.M.L & Linden, 1995). The study discussed that the use of traditional medicine is a primitive and indigenous method that was passed on from ancestors of people from West Africa, who lacked fundamental knowledge of mental illness cure that makes it harmful, ignorant and fallacious (Summerton, 2006; Ae-Ngibise et al., 2010). The study reported that the use of the traditional method to treat the mentally ill persons in West Africa is because of the availability, affordability, and accessibility (Ae-Ngibise, 2010; Opare-Henaku, 2013), and supernatural belief of people from West Africa (Barke, Nyarko & Klecha 2011). The study maintained that some traditional healers use voodoo to treat their mentally ill clients (Nwoko, 2009), while some use herbs, plants, and animals or divination to communicate with deities in the cure of the mentally ill person (Kpobi, Swartz, Omenyo, 2018).

The scarcity of medicine and uneven distribution of the little available medicine is also responsible for the use of traditional medicine for mental illness treatment (Ofori-Atta, A.M.L & Linden, 1995; Ae-Ngibise et al., 2010). Many of the mental health centers are in urban areas, so rural areas that are mostly affected by mental illness, seek treatment with traditional healers (Ae-Ngibise et al., 2010). Some people see the traditional medicine used in the treatment of mental illness in West Africa as fetish rituals that lack standard (Nwoko, 2009).

The study discussed the rise in the use of religion or prayer to cure mental illness in West Africa. It attributed the religious method of mental illness treatment as a result of the rise in Pentecostalism and Charismatic movements in West Africa. The study mentioned the use of holy water, prayers, fasting, and prophesying, anointed oils, and salts during the prayer of exorcism for mental illness cure (Kpobi, Swartz, Omenyo, 2018).

The World Health Organization (WHO) discussed that mental illness is the third leading cause of disease in the world, especially in Africa. The statistics say that about one in 7 children and adolescents in West Africa have mental health difficulties, and 1 in 10 persons experience the psychiatric disorder. The Center for Disease Control (CDC, 2010) also reported that African accounts are the highest level of depression (12.8%) in the world. The study revealed that the rates of mental illness in countries of West Africa correspond to the total number of mental illness in the world, and it accounts for the neglect in terms of diagnosis and treatment of those diagnosed with mental illness in West Africa.

The study discussed the reason for the use of exorcism and prayers to heal those with mental illness. This perception or idea comes from the rise of Pentecostalism, the Charismatic, and the new age of "holy spirit" power as a way of deliverance and healing (Luke 4: 33-37. It is the emergence of many religious prayer groups and the zeal to win souls that come with the new surge in prayer. The study equally noted that many of those with mental illness in West Africa seek treatment with traditional healers who may use sorcery to cast out assumed "demons" responsible for the person's mental illness.

The use of traditional healers in West Africa is still based on ancestral practices that follow the terrible and primitive ideas of healing mental illness (Ae-Ngibise et al., 2010). The study discussed that the difference between the traditional healers and the faith healers is that the traditional healers use herbs and libation while faith healers use prayers to treat mental illness (Puckree et al., 2002; Ae-Ngibise et al., 2010). The problem identified with some religious houses involved in the treatment of the mentally sick is that they may also use physical restraints to prevent the mentally ill in their captivity from escape. Some mentally ill may be tied with ropes on both hands, ankles, and back to prevent escape (Asuni, 1990), and they may be asked to go around asking for alms, singing, and dancing in the street (Asuni, 1990).

The study of cultural perception of mental illness in West Africa reported that education plays a vital role in decreasing stigmatization against the mentally ill person. The result of the study showed that the higher the training, the less the level of stigmatization against the mentally ill persons. The study discussed that the most significant cause of the negative perception against the mentally ill persons is due to lack of education. The observation is that in West Africa, inadequate or lack of proper knowledge leads to poor understanding of mental illness prognosis, types, diagnoses, and treatment. Also, a lack of education on mental illness is the reason persons with mental illness in West Africa flock to the traditional healers for treatment (Ae-Ngibise et al., 2010). The study reiterated the need for conventional and faith healers to go for training or get adequate education on human rights issues and effective treatment modalities. It was also observed in the study that culture, social, and economic factors are responsible for the high patronage of traditional medicine in West Africa (Ae-Ngibise et al., 2010).

The study argued that the inadequacy of the public health sector in West Africa is responsible for the poor knowledge of mental illness disorder and contributes to the poor treatment given to the mentally ill person (Gureje & Lasebikan, (2006). The governments in West Africa are not doing enough to invest more resources in mental illness treatment, and good government policy and the human right profession will help to decrease stereotypes and discrimination against mental illness (Walker, 2015). The governments in West Africa are also encouraged to train state community health workers to assist in creating awareness about mental illness in West Africa (Easton et al., 2007).

The study discussed that mental illness is considered of low priority in West African countries because of the government focus on the eradication of poverty first. It is because of the low priority on mental illness eradication that the civil society organization (CSO) should be involved to play an important advocacy role on mental illness issues, and to change the negative attitude on mental illness in West Africa (Omar et al., 2010). The use of international policy stakeholders is to participate in areas of finance to create mental illness awareness in West Africa (Omar et al., 2010). The study reiterated the need for West African governments and agencies to take a look on ways to end stigmatization and discrimination against mentally ill persons, through the provision of financial assistance, counseling, proper medical treatment, and support to families of a mentally ill person in caring for their mentally sick ones.

Findings

The finding of this study is that "lack of love" is the primary reason mentally ill persons are stigmatized or stereotyped in West Africa. The study found that most mentally sick persons are denied food, shelter, clothing, and medical care. It is the denial of the basic needs of life that makes some mentally ill persons run away from their homes, and roam about the streets looking for food in trash bags. It was found through the data analyses and the interviewing of participants that love or compassion can be used to improve mental illness treatment in West Africa. The fact that the mentally ill persons are abandoned and not allowed to stay in the same house with healthy persons creates anger within them.

The study noted that most mentally ill persons are chained and bitten with a cane, and left in the open 24 hours a day with rain and sun beating them. The reason for chaining the mentally ill by family members is to prevent them from going out of the family house. So chaining the mentally ill person hinders their freedom and expression of their mind, and subsequently leads to anger and aggression. The fear of being attacked or beaten with a cane or chained also makes the mentally sick persons run away from their house. It is the same fear of being attacked or beaten that makes some mentally ill persons dangerous and can retaliate against attack by other people. Most of the mentally ill persons are without food, which leaves them to scavenge for food in trash bags. People also avoid the mentally sick persons and sometimes spit and throw stones to them. It is the denials of the basic amenities, like foods, shelter, and love, and the stigma attached to mental illness that create anger among the mentally ill persons.

Another finding from the study is that lack of education on mental illness is the primary barrier to treatment. Many people from West Africa do not know what causes mental illness or different types of mental illness. The type of mental illness perceived mostly as mad people are those with psychosis or hallucination. The finding noted that education is the essential piece to remove stigmatization against mental illness in West Africa, and it should start from the primary school age to the university.

There is also a finding that culture influences West African perception of mental illness. It is the cultural perception that brought about the opinion that demons or evil spirit attacks cause mental illness in West Africa. It is the demonizing understanding of mental illness that makes the mentally ill avoid going for treatment in West

Africa. Also, the negative mindset that originated from the ancestors of people from West Africa about mental illness has continued to be the perception of mental illness up to the present time.

Another finding is that governments in West Africa are not doing enough to curtail the negative perception of mental illness. The result of the study shows that only 2% of approved health resources for mental illness were used, and these might be due to corruption by governments in West Africa. Another finding from the study is that the resources approved for mental illness are often utilized in the cities, while the rural areas with more mentally ill persons are left with no resources.

The finding from the study also shows that stigmatization affects the mentally ill persons and their families. It was the result of the stigma against family members that makes people abandon their family member with mental illness. The finding also shows that people avoid marrying from families of a mentally ill person because of the fear that mental illness is infectious and transferrable.

The findings suggest that if the mentally ill persons are provided food, shelter, and clothing, with proper treatment, mental illness will decrease in West Africa. The result of the study also shows that discriminating against the mentally ill persons from interacting with friends and community members creates social stigmatization that makes them unstable to discuss or share anything with others, and it subsequently creates anger and loneliness on the mentally ill person. The study found out that mentally ill persons are not allowed to get employment, so it makes them unable to care for themselves, except depending on others to provide their needs. The study calls for more research on mental illness diagnosis, stigmatization, and stereotypes in West Africa, and more emphasis should focus on the use of education to eradicate mental illness negative perception in West Africa.

Recommendations

Strongest among our few recommendations here is the fact that the governments in West Africa should;

1. Get involved in literacy campaign to educate their people on mental illness causes and treatments, and by using media outlets and in schools to create mental illness awareness;

2. More psychiatric health and rehabilitation centers should be established to treat those diagnosed with mental illness, especially in the rural areas of the country;

3. The governments and other agencies should also provide resources to feed and accommodate those with mental health issues in West Africa;

4. More mental health personnel should be trained to bring mental illness awareness to the people of West Africa. On the same par, it will be consequential and beneficial to train mental health professionals on cultural competences before being sent to work with mentally ill persons from another culture;

5. Also, community' centers, churches and various traditional families/believers should be used to bring mental illness awareness to the grassroots;

6. Stigmatization against the mentally ill should be discouraged or banned to improve health outcome.

Table 11: Two Types of Stigmatization against Mentally ill Persons:

Public Stigma	Self-Stigma
➤ **Stereotypes** Negative thought by others as: ▪ Dangerous ▪ Incompetent ▪ Stupid ▪ Mad ➤ **Prejudice:** Negative Emotion Reaction with Belief: e.g., anger, Fear ➤ **Discrimination:** e.g. Job denial Housing denial	➤ **Stereotypes** Negative thought about self as: ▪ Weak ▪ Incompetent ▪ Low self-esteem ➤ **Prejudice:** Negative Emotion Reaction against self: e.g. Low self-esteem Low self-efficacy ➤ **Discrimination:** e.g. Unwillingness to look for job

Table 12: Summary of Results on Mental Illness in West Africa

Themes	Consequences	Interventions.
Stigmatization ➤ Internal Stigma ➤ External Stigma	Self-Hatred and low self-esteem • Stigma from health care workers and mental health centers. • Lack of proper treatment from mental health workers.	1. Education for mentally ill person, family and community members. 2. Use of media outlet like radio, TV and bill boards to create awareness of mental illness.

	• Neglect, beaten, ridiculed from family members.	3. School education starting from the primary to tertiary institutions about mental illness prevention.
	• Denial of basic amenities like food, housing and clothing.	4. Improved government policy on mental illness diagnose and treatment.
	• Tied to the tree and not allowed to stay inside the house.	5. Improvement of traditional methods of healing.
	• Community labeling of mentally ill as mad, idiot and useless.	6. Support from families and the society on mental illness prevention.
	• Social and structural discrimination in getting a job and associating with health people.	7. Advocacy for the mentally ill persons in West Africa.
	• Lack of government incentives and funding.	8. Psycho-education to aid recovery and empower mentally ill individuals and their family members
➢ Causes of mental illness	▪ Caused by witchcraft attack, curses, drug use, wars, parental curses, and God's punishment.	
➢ Effects of Stigma on mental illness	▪ Poor health and untimely death	

CHAPTER SIX

WORK YET TO BE DONE

Limitations

The small size of participants (n=18), without the intervention of the sampled participants, in the study may not have represented the accurate cultural perception of mental illness in West Africa. The fundamental 18 participants utilized in the study may not have been enough to totally help us understand mental illness perception, stigma, and stereotypes against mental illness in West Africa. The limited number of participants used in the study may also not have represented the general population perception of mental illness in West Africa, and it could affect the reliability of the study. The normally sound participant's level of understanding of the scope of mental illness in West Africa might be unrealistic because of their absence in the country for extended period of time. Some participants were unaware of the different types of mental illnesses, but viewed mental illness only on the sides and signs of psychosis or hallucination. Mental illnesses like anger, minor depression, attention deficit disorder, etc. are not perceived as mental illness by most people from West Africa. The perception is that only the mentally ill persons are aimlessly seen walking on the street or tied on a tree or has psychosis and hallucination is sick mentally, whereas our study here revealed that every normal human being has some percentage of madness.

Besides, another limitation on this study of mental illness is the problem of "cultural diffusion" as a result of many years of absence in West Africa. The cultural diffusion may prevent people from understanding the difference between western culture and that of West African people. Some of the participants may have forgotten the real negative perceptions and stigma against mentally ill persons or current issues about mental illness perception in West Africa. It is possible that those who recorded the stigma and stereotypes against the mentally ill may have been away for a long time from West Africa and may not know of any new changes in the perception or stereotype against the mentally ill in West Africa.

Again, some of our participants were not very open to discuss mental illness issues due to cultural taboos of sharing perceived family or cultural aspects of their country. Some participants felt that addressing the mental illness of their culture could signify a betrayal or some sort of backwardness against their tribe. Thus, some of them tended to be skeptical sharing details of their cultures on mental illness. Some participants also viewed mentally ill persons as worthless in society, so it did not warrant wasting their time discussing various aspects of it in public.

A huge limitation of the study centered on the fact that some Muslim women's' unwillingness to participate in the study due to religious and cultural connotation. Some Muslim women do not discuss with men based on their religion, let alone to speak on such issues without their husband's consent. Though, we noted that religion may play a part in participant's decision to discuss mental illness, especially on how it is perceived, but it vital to note that some religions may be protective in discussing how mentally ill persons are seen or treated in West Africa. The participants utilized in the study were basically those from two religions – Christianity and Muslim. In this instance, as long as the perception of the traditionalist or native religion was not seriously considered, it is a limitation in a search that should have involved all strata and branches of religions. The non-representation of all faith in the study may hinder the accurate understanding of mental illness in West Africa. Thus, it is a limitation also.

As could be ascertained from our scope, the study was conducted in Philadelphia and may not have reflected the perceptions of all West African people around the globe. The participants in the study were chosen from 10 out of the 15 countries in West Africa, which may not have adequately reflected the opinions of all cultures in West Africa. What a limitation? There are many other cultures within the 10 participants' countries that were not covered in the study. In a country like Nigeria, there are over 250 dialectical languages and cultures. Unfortunately, only two cultures were represented in the survey. The general effects of the impact of hunger, poverty, and stresses was not measured or limited in the understanding of the effect or contribution to mental illness in West Africa, normal people are equally involved. The concentration of the study on mentally ill persons majorly in the rural areas of West African countries, mainly with participants who have lived in the urban areas, and not know much about mental illness stigma or stereotypes in West Africa, was not the best.

All the same, the study of mental illness perception in West Africa required more research to investigate the perceived stereotypes, stigma, and negative perception of mentally ill persons, through the lens of different religious and cultural groups in West Africa. In other words, our present study has fired the hardest shot, and expects other studies of mental illness create more awareness on the areas of education and people from West Africa as to assist in decreasing stigmatization and stereotypes against mental illness. Our studies harmed more on the need for more government involvement through provision of adequate health care facilities for mental illness treatment, but local government headquarters should have been asked to play their own major roles. Asking the governments in West Africa to take a clue from western countries to create counseling and treatment centers, and welfare services that will assist in the provision of medications, food, clothing and shelter to improve wellbeing of the mentally ill persons, may sound insulting. But the reality is there, especially when rich West African countries selfishly waste their resources in frivolities and political inordinate ambitions.

The implication of the study

The study of cultural perception of mental illness provided evidence of traumas experienced by mentally ill people in West Africa, and the effects on their families. The study brought to awareness the neglect in treating people diagnosed with mental illness because of the negative perception that mental illness is infections, transferable, or associated with 'demons.' The negative perception of mental illness resulted in discrimination, social avoidance, structural stigma, and different forms of abuses against the mentally ill person. The implication of the social avoidance negatively resulted in denial of the mentally ill person's from receiving adequate care, communication, and socialization with others in the society. It shows that the mentally ill persons are not seen as human beings but as useless people that have no worth in the community. But the research calls for reorientations to accommodate them as fellow citizens.

The mentally ill persons are also stigmatized against by health care workers like the psychiatrists, nurses, and social workers in West Africa. The result of the stigma by mental health workers against the mentally ill persons shows that they may not get proper diagnoses or care or the right medications for treatment. Hereby, there is need for workers' reorientations too.

The study of cultural perception of mental illness in West Africa shows that there are perceived myths about mental illness that are not true. It is the belief in these myths that possess a problem in the acceptance and treatment of the mentally ill persons. Some of the myths about mental illness include that it is incurable, and the mentally ill are dangerous to live or work with. These tales have led to non-acceptance of the mentally ill to work with an organization or any agency. The effect of the non-acceptance of the mentally ill in workplaces also leads to unavailability of funds to seek proper medical treatment, and it may lead to patronizing of quacks for mental illness treatment. It is the negative perception and stigma against the mentally ill that forms the health seeking behavior of those with mental illness in West Africa, and patronizing of traditional healers for treatment.

The implication of stigma and negative perception against mental illness may lead to high rate of morbidity and mortality of the mentally ill person's in West Africa. It is through eating from the trash bags that most mentally sick inwardly contract disease that leads to their untimely death, which eventually contributes to their untimely deaths. The mentally ill persons that are chained and left on the open day and night might contact diseases that could also lead to their untimely death, is also inhumanity to man. Some mentally ill in West Africa are sometimes seen sleeping in bushes which could endanger their lives from attack by wild animals. The implication implies that workforce is wasted by not treating those with mental illness in West Africa to contribute to the economy.

The perception of mental illness in West Africa is still through the lens of the primitive cultural ideology of their ancestors who never experienced technological development that mental illness is curable. The significance of the ignorant cultural perception calls for education of West African people to understand the causes, type, diagnosis, and treatment of mental illness. The use of knowledge will also assist in decreasing the stereotypes and stigma against the mentally ill persons in West Africa. The implication is that other interventions like utilizing religious institutions, local health care workers, schools, and media can be improved to create awareness of mental illness and decrease stigma against the mentally ill in West Africa. The use of education will also help people from West Africa to understand mental illness causes, and other treatment options like biogenic medications and counseling available to treat mental illness. Educating people from West Africa about mental illness will help create awareness on the negative impact of culture on mental illness that is not true, as to discard the negative perception on mental illness.

The study implies that it will help governments in West Africa to foster a more positive way to improve mental illness treatment, and to approve more funds for its treatment. The creation of the mental health department in the department of health of each country in West Africa will also be essential to monitor and implement measures to improve the welfare of those diagnosed with mental illness. The traditional healers will also be educated to understand how wrong dosages application can hurt mental illness treatment. The classic and faith healers can learn that mentally ill persons also have self-rights that should not be abused. The governments in West Africa can incorporate traditional healers into one body to monitor abuses and improve patients care.

The study discourages the use of a cane, chaining, and food denial as a way of punishment for the mentally ill in West Africa. Also, the use of medication can be utilized to treat mentally ill people with psychosis, hallucination, and major depression. More research will be needed to understand mental illness perception, stigma, and stereotypes through the cultural lens of people from West Africa, and to explore religious and spiritual effects of treating people with mental illness in West Africa. Also, more research will be necessary to understand the use of traditional medicine to cure mental illness in West Africa. There should be ongoing studies in this field!

Table 13: Summary of Limitations on the Study:

a. Small size of participants (n=18+others)	g. Some religion not allowing their women to speak in the public without the husband consent;
b. Participants may have unrealistic current perception of mental illness in West Africa;	h. Only Christians and Muslims participated in the study;
c. Ignorant of different types of mental illness;	i. Study was conducted in Philadelphia with 10 out of 15 countries in West Africa;
d. Only psychosis and hallucination persons are seen as mentally ill;	j. More research is needed to understand the impact of spirituality on mental illness.
e. Cultural diffusion of participant's culture due to long absence from West Africa;	
f. Cultural taboo to discuss mental illness in some cultures;	

Table 14: Summary of Implication of the Study:

a. The study brought into awareness the negative perception of mental illness in West Africa as caused by "demons", "Witchcraft", "curses" and "drugs";. b. Mentally ill person's denial of adequate care, socialization with others causes more harm and alienation against mentally ill person; c. Curable mental illnesses are not treated and they result to untimely death; d. Lack of mental illness facilities results in patronizing traditional healers who are ignorant of mental illness cure;	e. People from West Africa still believe on their ancestor's primitive ideology on mental illness; f. The study creates awareness that the use of education can be used to decrease stigmatization against mentally ill persons; g. Schools and media can be sources to be used in decreasing mental illness stereotypes and stigma; h. Governments and stakeholders can contribute to improve mental illness treatment in West Africa.

CHAPTER SEVEN

BIBLIOGRAPHY AND SOURCES

—⁓—

Abdulmalik J, Fadahunsi W, Kola L, Nwefoh E, Minas H, Eaton J, Gureje O. (2014). The Mental Health Leadership and Advocacy Program (mhLAP): a pioneering response to the neglect of mental health in Anglophone West Africa. *International Journal of Mental Health Systems,*8:5.

Achiga, L. C., (2016). A new perspective on mental illness: From Nigeria to SW United States, *Issues in Mental Health Nursing,* 37.5, 367-371

Adewuya, A., & Oguntade, A. (2007).Doctors' attitude towards people with mental illness in Western Nigeria. *Social Psychiatry and Psychiatric Epidemiology,* 42(11), 931-936

Adewuya, A.O. & Makanjuola, R. O. (2008).Social distance towards people with mental illness in Southwestern Nigeria. *Australian and New Zealand Journal of Psychiatry,* 42: 389-395

Ae-Ngibisi, K., Cooper, S., Adibokah, E., Akpalu, B., Lund, C., Doku, V. & MHAPP Research Program Consortium. (2010). Whether you like it or not people with mental problems are going to go to them: *A qualitative exploration into the provision of mental health care in Ghana. International Review of Psychiatry,* 22(6), 558-567

Ae-Ngibise, K., Doku, V. C., Asante, K.P. & Owusu-Agyei, S. (2015). The experience of caregivers of people living with serious mental disorders: a study from rural Ghana. *Global Health Action*

Afe, T. O., Bello-Mojeed, M. & Ogunsemi, O. (2016).Perception of Service Satisfaction and Quality of Life of Patients Living with Schizophrenia in Lagos, Nigeria. *Journal of Neurosciences in Rural Practice*, 7:216-222

Akotia, C.S., Knizek, B.L., Kinnyanda, E. & Hjelmeland, H. (2014). I have sinned: Understanding the role of religion in the experiences of suicide attempters in Ghana. *Mental Health, Religion and Culture*, vol. 17, No. 5, 437-448

Al-Krenawi, A., Graham, J.R. (1997). Spirit possession and exorcism: the integration of modern and traditional mental health care systems in the treatment of a Bedouin patient. *Clinical Social Work Journal,* 25: 211-222

Alvarez, R. A., Feaster, D. J., Mayorga, C. C., Mitrani, V. B., & Vasquez, E. (2006). Increasing minority research participation through community organization research. *Western Journal of Nursing Research*, 28(5), 561-563.

Agyapong, V.I; Osei, K; Farren, C.K. & McAuliffe, E. (2015). Task Shifting-Ghana's Community Mental Health Workers experiences and perceptions of their roles and scope of practice. *Department of Psychiatry*. Global Health Action.

Asamoah, M.k., Osafo, J., Agyapong, I. (2014). The Role of Pentecostal Clergy in Mental Health- Care Delivery in Ghana. *Mental Health, Religion and Culture*, Vol. 17(6), 601-614

Asanter, K., Meyer-Weitz, A. & Peterson, I. (2016). Mental health and health risk behaviors of homeless adolescents and youths: A mixed methods study. *Child Youth Care Forum*, 45:433-449.

Asuni, T. (1990). Nigeria: Report on the care treatment and rehabilitation of people with mental illness. *Psychological Rehabilitation Journal*.

Aremeyaw, A.A. (2013). *Anas returns with the messiah of Mentukwa.* Retrieved February 9, 2019, from http://edition.myjoyonline. com/pages/news.

Asamoah-Gyadu, J. K. (2013) Contemporary Pentecostal Christianity: Interpretations from an African context, Oxford: Regnum Books.

Ashton, C. M., Haidet, P., Paterniti, D.A., Collins, T.C., Gordon, H.S., O'Malley, K, Street, R.L. Jr. (2003). Racial and ethnic disparities in the use of health services: Bias, preferences, or poor communication? *Journal of General Internal Medicine*, 18, 146-152.

Atindanbila S. & Thompson C.E. (2011).The role of African traditional healers in the management of mental challengesin Africa. *Journal of Emerging Trends in Educational Research and Policy Studies*, 2(6), 457-464

Augsburger, D. (1986). Pastoral counseling across cultures: theological studies, Philadelphia, Westminster, vol. (49(, 195 – 197

Barke, A., Nyarko, S. & Klecha, D. (2011). The stigma of mental illness in Southern Ghana: Attitudes of the urban population and patients views. *Social Psychiatry and Psychiatry Epidemiology*, 46, 1191-1202

Bella-Awusah, T; Adedokun, B; Dogra, N. & Omigbodun, O. (2014). The impact of a mental health teaching program on rural and urban secondary school students perceptions of mental illness in southwest Nigeria. *Journal of Child and Adolescent Mental Health*, 26(3): 207-215

Bhui, K., Rudell, K., & Priebe, S. (2006). Assessing explanatory models for common mental disorders. *Journal of Clinical Psychiatry*, 67, 964-971

Biswas, J., Gangadhar, B.N., & Keshavan. (2016). Cross cultural variations in psychiatrists perception of mental illness: A tool for teaching culture in psychiatry. *Asian Journal of Psychiatry*, 23: 1-7

Braun, V., & Clarke, V. (2006).Using thematic analysis in psychology. *Qualitative Research in Psychology, 3*(2), 77–101.

Brohan E, Gauci, D. Sartorius N. K. & Thornicroft G. (2011). Self-stigma, empowerment and perceived discrimination among people with bipolar disorder or depression in 13 European Countries. The GAMIAN- Europe Study. *Journal of Affective Disorders*, 129, 56-63

Browne, K. (2007). Snowball sampling: Using social networks to research non-heterosexual women. *International Journal of Social Research Methodology*, vol. 8, p. 47-60

Bukola, S., Jordana, S., Hegadoren, K. (2019). Access and Utilization of mental health services for immigrants and refugees: Perspective of immigrants service providers. International *Journal of Mental Health Nursing*, vol. 28(1) 152- 161

Campbell-Hall, V., Petersen, I., Bhana, A., Mjadu, S., Flisher, H.V., A.J. & MHaPP Research Programme Consortium. (2010). Collaboration between traditional practitioners and primary health care staff in South Africa: developing a workable partnership for community mental health services. *Transcultural psychiatry*, 47(4), 610-628

Carrel, A. (1935). Man, the unknown. New York, *Harper and Bros Press*, p. 319

Chong, S.A., Verna, S., Vaingankar, J.A., Chan, Y.H., Wong, L.Y. & Heng, B.H. (2007).Perceptions of public towards the mentally ill in a developed Asian Country. *Social Psychiatry and Psychiatric Epidemiology*, 42, 734 – 739

Coleman, R., Morison, L., Paine, K., Powell, R.A. & Walraven, G. (2006).Women reproductive health and depression. A community survey in Gambia, West Africa. *Social Psychiatry and Psychiatric Epidemiology*, 41: 720-727.

Corrigan, P., & Miller, F. (2004). Shame, blame, and contamination: A review of the impact of the mental illness stigma on family members. *Journal of Mental Health*, 13(6), 537-548.

Corrigan, P.W. & Watson, A.C. (2002).The paradox of self-stigma and mental illness. *Clinical Psychology*, 9:35-53

Dako-Gyeke, M. & Asumang, E.S. (2013). Stigmatization and discrimination experiences of persons with mental illness: Insights from a qualitative study in Southern Ghana. *Social Work Soc.* 11(1):1-14

Decruyenaere, M., Evers-Kiebooms, G., Welkenhuysen, M., Denayer, L., & Claes, E. (2000). Cognitive representations of breast cancer, emotional distress and preventive health behavior: a theoretical perspective. *Psycho-oncology*, 9, 528-536

Doku, P.N. & Minnis, H. (2016).Multi-informant perspective on psychological distress among Ghanaians orphans and vulnerable children within the context of HIV/AIDS. *Psychological Medicine*, 46, 2329-2336.

Duthé, G., Rossier, C., Bonnet, D., Soura, A. B., & Corker, J. (2016). Mental health and urban living in sub-Saharan Africa: major depressive episodes among the urban poor in Ouagadougou, Burkina Faso. *Population Health Metrics*, *14*, 18.

Eaton, J., Nwefoli, E., Okafor, G., Onyeonoro, U., Nwaubani, K. & Henderson, C. (2017).Interventions to Increase the Use of Services; Mental Health Awareness in Nigeria. *International Journal of Mental Health*, 11:66

Ebuenyi, I.D., Syurina, E.V., Bunders, J.F. & Regeer, B.J. (2018). Barriers to and facilitators of employment for people with psychotic disabilities in Africa: a coping review. *Global Health Action*, vol. 11

Egbe, C.O., Brooke-Summer, C., Kathree, T., Selohilwe, O., Thomicroft, & Petersen, I. (2014). Psychiatric stigma and discrimination in South Africa: perspective from key stakeholders. *BMC Psychiatry*, 14: 191

Elkonin, D., Brown, O. & Naicker, S. (2012). Religion, Spirituality and Therapy: Implications for Training. *Journal of Religious Health*, 53: 119-134

Flick, U., Kardorff, E. & Steirike (2004). A companion to qualitative research; *Osage Publication*

Furnham, A., & Murao, M. (2000). A cross cultural comparison of British and Japanese lay theories of schizophrenia. *International journal of social psychology*, 46, 4-20

Gaebel, W., Zaske, H., Cleveland, H. R., Zielasek, J., Stuart, H., Arboleda-Florez, J., Akiyama, T., Gureja, O., Jorge, M. R., Kastrup, M., Suzuki, Y., Tasman, A. & Sartorius, N. (2011).Measuring the Stigma of Psychiatry and Psychiatrists: *Development of a Questionnaire. Europe Arch Psychiatry Clinical Neurosis*, 261(2), 119-123

Green E. (1999). Engaging indigenous African healers in the prevention of AIDS and STDs. In R.Hahn(Ed.).*Anthropology in Public Health*, 63-83. London Oxford University Press

Gur, K., Sener, N., Kucuk, L., Cetindag, Z. & Basar, M. (2012). The beliefs of teachers towards mental illness.*Procedia – Social and Behavioral Sciences*, 47, 1146-1152

Gureje, O., Lasebikan, V., Ephraim-Oluwanuga, O., Olley, B., & Kola, L. (2005). Community study of knowledge of and attitude to mental illness in Nigeria. *The British Journal of Psychiatry*, 186(5), 436-441.

Gureje O. & Lasebikan V. (2006).Use of mental health services in a developing country. *Social Psychiatry and Psychiatric Epidemiology*, 4(1), 44-49

Gureje, O., Olley, B., Olusola, F. & Kola, L. (2006). Do beliefs about causation influence attitudes to mental illness. *World Psychiatry*, 5: 104-107

Gyamfi, S; Hegadoren, K. & Park, T. (2018).Individual factors that influence experiences and perceptions of stigma and discrimination towards people with mental illness in Ghana. *International Journal of Mental Health Nursing*, 368-377

Hadley, C., Tegegn, A., Tessema, F., Asefa, M. & Galea, S. (2008). Parental symptoms of common mental disorders and children's social motor and language development in Sub-Saharan African. *Annals of Human Biology*, 35(3): 259-275

Ibrahim, A., Hor, S., Bahar, O.S., Dwomoh, D., Mckay, M., Esena, R. & Agyeponge, I.A. (2016). Pathways to psychiatric care for mental disorder: a retrospective study of patients seeking mental health services at a public psychiatric facility in Ghana. *International Journal of Mental Health Systems,* 10:63

Iheanacho, T., Obiefune, M., Ezeanolue, C., Ogedegbe, G., Nwanyanwu, C., Ehiri, J., Ohaeri, J. & Ezeanolue, E. (2015). Integrating mental health screening into routine community maternal and child health activity: experience from prevention of mother-to-child HIV transmission (PMTCT) trial in Nigeria, *Social Psychiatry epidemiology*, 50: 489-495

Ismayilova, L; Karimili, L; Sanson, J; Gaveras, E; Nanema, R; To-Camier, A; Chaffin, J. (2018). Improving Mental health among ultra-poor children. Two year outcomes of a cluster-randomized trial in Burkina Faso. *Social Science and Medicine*, Vol. 208, p. 180-189

Jack, H., Caravan, M., Bradley, E. & Ofori-Atta, A. (2015). Aggression in mental health settings: a case study in Ghana; *Bulletin of World Health Organization*, 93(8).

James, B.O., Igbinomwanhia, N. G., & Omoaregba. (2014). Clergy as collaborators in the delivery of mental health care: An exploratory survey from Benin City Nigeria, *Transcultural Psychiatry*, 51(4) 569 – 580

Kabir, M., Iliyasu, Z., Abubakar, I. S. & Aliyu, M.H. (2004). Perceptions and Beliefs about Mental Illness among Adults in Karfi Village, Northern Nigeria. *BMC International Health and Human Rights*, 4:3

Kadri N, Manoudi, F, Berrada, S. & Moussaouui, D. (2004).Stigma impact on Moroccan families of patients with Schizophrenia. *Canadian Journal of Psychiatry*, 49, 625-629

Kessler, R., Nelson, C., Mckinagle, K.,Edlund, M., Frank, R. & Leaf, P. (1996). The epidemiology of co-occurring additive and mental disorders: Implications for prevention and service utilization. *American journal of orthopsychiatry*, 66, 17 – 31

Kim, H. W. & Salyers, M.P. (2008). Attitudes and Perceived Barriers to working with families of persons with severe mental illness: Mental Health Professional Perspectives. *Community Mental Health*, 44:337-345

Kinsinger F. S. (2009). Beneficence and the professional's moral imperative. *Journal of chiropractic humanities*, *16*(1), 44–46.

Klik, K.A., William, S.L, & Reynolds, K. (2019). Towards understanding mental illness stigma and help-seeking: A social identity perspective

Kohrt, B.A. (2015). Adapting the crisis intervention team (CIT) model of Police-Mental health collaboration in a low-income post conflict country: Curriculum development in Liberia West Africa. *American Journal of Public Health*, vol. 105 (3).

Koramoa, J; Lynch, M.A. & Kinnair, D. (2002). A continuum of child-rearing: responding to traditional practice; *Child Abuse Review*, vol. (11), 415-421

Kpabi, L; Swartz, L. (2018). That is how the real mad people behave. Beliefs about and treatment of mental disorders by traditional medicine men in Accra, Ghana. *International Journal of Social Psychiatry*, Vol. 64(4), p. 309-316

Kpabi, L; Swartz, L. & Omenyo, C. (2018).Traditional methods of treating mental disorders in Ghana. *Journal Indexing and Matrix*, vol. 56(1).

Kruk, M. E., Rockers, P. C., William, E. H., Varpilah, S.T., Macauley, R., Saydee, G. & Galea, S. (2010). Availability of essential health services in post-conflict Liberia. *Bull World Health Organization*, 88: 527-534

Kushitor, M.K., Peterson, M.B., Asante, P.Y., Dodoo, N. D., Boatemaa, S., Awuah, R. B., De-Graft Aikins, A. (2018). Community and individual sense of trust and psychological distress among the urban poor in Accra Ghana. *PloS ONE*, 13(9), 1-13

Kyei, J. J., Dueck, A., Indart, M.J., Nyarko, N.Y. (2014). Supernatural belief systems, mental health and perceptions of mental disorders in Ghana; *International Journal of Culture and Mental Health,* Vol. 7(2) p. 137-151

Lartey, E. (2003). Approach to pastoral care in pluralistic settings, a *Journal of Pastoral Theology*

Lefley, H.P. (1990). Rehabilitation in mental illness: Insights from other cultures. *Psychological Rehabilitation Journal*, vol. 14

Leong, F. T & Kim, H. (2001). Going beyond cultural sensitivity, on the road to multiculturalism: using the intercultural sensitizer as a counselor training tool: *Journal of Counseling and Development*, Vol. 70.

Liegghio, M. (2017). Not a good person: Family stigma of mental illness from the perspective of young siblings. *Child and Family Social Work*, 22: 1237-1245

Link, B.G., Yang, L.H., Phehan, J.C. & Collins, P.Y. (2004). Measuring mental illness stigma. Retrieved from http:// schizophreniabulletin.oxfordjournals.org on May, 17th 2019.

Lund, C., Myer. L., Stein, D. J., Williams, D. R., & Flisher, A.J. (2013).Mental illness and lost income among adult South African. *Social Psychiatry and Psychiatric Epidemiology*, 48(5), 845-851.

Mak, W.S., Chong, E.K., & Wong, C.Y.(2014). Beyond attributions: Understanding public stigma of mental illness with the common sense model. *American Journal of Orthopsychiatry*, 84(2)-173-181.

Makanjuola, A.B., Adelekan, M. L., & Morakinyo, O. O. (2000). The current status of traditional mental health practice in Ilorin emirate council area, Kwara State Nigeria. West African *Journal of Medicine*, 19(1), 43-49

Makanjuola, V., Essan, Y., Oladeji, B., Kola, L., Appiah-Poku, J., Harris, B., Othieno, C., Price, L., Seedat, S. & Gureje, O. (2016). Explanatory Model of Psychosis: *Impact on Perceptions of Self-Stigma by Patients in Three Sub-Saharan African Cities. Social Psychiatry and Epidemiology*, 51:1645-1654

Mechanic, D. (1999). Mental health and mental illness: Definitions and perspectives. In A. V. Horwitz & T. L. Scheid (Eds.), *A handbook for the study of mental health: Social contexts, theories, and systems* (pp. 12-28). New York, NY, US: Cambridge University Press.

Melinda, A. & Sharp, M. (2007). A review of Emmanuel Y. Lartey's post colonializing God: An *African Practical Theology*, 66 (143-145).

Mfoafo-M'Carthy, M., Sottie, C. & Gyan, C. (2016). Mental illness and stigma: a 10-year review of portrayal through print media in Ghana (2003 – 2012): *journal of culture and mental health,*

Monteiro, N.M. & Balogun S. K. (2014). Perceptions of mental illness in Ethiopia: A profile of attitudes, beliefs and practices among community members, healthcare workers and traditional healers. *International Journal of Culture and Mental Health,* 7, 259-272.

Noble, H. & Smith, J. (2015).Issues of Validity and Reliability in Qualitative Research. *Evidence Based Nursing,* 18:34-35

Nwoko, K.C. (2009). Traditional psychiatric healing in Igbo Land, Southeastern Nigeria. *African Journal History Culture,* 1(2):036-043

Oduguwa, A. O., Adedokun, B. & Omigbodun, O. O. (2017).Effect of a mental health training program on Nigeria school pupil's perceptions of mental illness. *Child and Adolescent Psychiatry and Mental Health,* 11:19

O'Grady, K. A; White, K. & Schreiber-Pan, H. (2015). Cross-cultural counseling: the importance of encountering the liminal space, *Springer Publishing.*

Olusina, A.K. & Ohaeri, J.U. (2003).Subjective Quality of Life of Recently Discharged Nigeria Psychiatric Patients. *Social Psychiatric Epidemiology,* 38: 707-714

Omar, M.A., Green, T.A., Bird, P.K., Mirzoer, T., Flisher, A.J., Kigozi, F., Lund, C., Nwanza, J., offori-Atta, A.L., Mental Health and Poverty Research Programme Consortium (mHaPP) (2010). Mental health policy process: a comparative study of Ghana, South Africa, Uganda and Zambia. *International Journal of Mental Health Systems,* 4:24

Onyencho, V.C., Omeiza, B. & Wakil, M. A. (2014).Post-traumatic stress disorder and psychological well-being among University of Maiduguri Students. *Ife Center for Psychological Studies*, 22(1), 195-201

Onyina O. (2002). Deliverance as a way of confronting witchcraft in modern Africa: Ghana as a case history. *Asian Journal of Pentecostal Studies*, 5, 107-134

Opare-Henaku, A. (2013). Notions of spirits as agents of mental illness among the Akan of Ghana: *A Cultural Psychological Explanation* (Retrieved April 11, 2019, from http://www. scholarscompass.vcu.edu.

Osafo, J. (2016). Seeking paths for collaboration between religious leaders and mental health professionals in Ghana. *Pastoral Psychology*, 65: 493-508

Osei A.O. (2001). Types of Psychiatric Illness at Traditional Healing Centers in Ghana. *Ghana Medical Journal*, 35, 106-110

Osei, Y. (1994). Psychiatric Service in a Developing Country - The Case of Ghana Curare, 17, 39-43

Owitti, J. A., Palinski, A., Ajaz, A., Ascoli, M., Jongh, B. & Bhui, K. (2015). Explanations of illness experiences among community mental health patients: An argument for the use of an ethnographic interview method in routine clinical care. *International review of psychiatry*, 27(1), 23-38

Padavachee, P.,& Laher, S. (2014). South African Hindu psychologists' perceptions of mental illness.*Journal of Religion and Health*, 53(2), 424-437.

Patel, V., Belkin, G.S., Chockalingam, A., Cooper, J., Saxena, S., Unutzer, J. (2013). Grand challenge integrating mental health services into priority health care platforms, *Plos med*, (5), 1-6

Patel, V; Eaton, J.,. Revista B. P., (2010).Principles to guide mental health policies in low- and middle-income countries, Vol. 32 (4), p343-344.

Picco, L., Pang, S., Lan, Y. W., Jeyagumnathan, A., Satghara, P., Abdin, E., Vaingankar, J.A., Lim, S., Poh, C.L. & Chong, M.S. (2016). Internalized stigma among psychiatric outpatients: Associations with quality of life, functioning, hope and self-esteem. *Psychiatry Research*, 246:500-506

Pigeon-Gagne, E., Hassan, G., Yaogo, M. & Ridde, V. (2017).An exploratory study assessing psychological distress of indigents in Burkina Faso. A step forward in understanding mental health needs in West Africa. *International Journal of Equity in Health*, 16:143

Puckree T, Mkhize, M, Mgobhozi, Z. & Lin J. (2002). African traditional healers: what healthcare professionals need to know. *International Journal of Rehabilitation Research*, 25, 247-251

Quinn N. (2007). Beliefs and community responses to mental illness in Ghana. The experience of family careers. *International Journal of Social Psychiatry*, 53, 175-188

Rahman A, Mubbasher M.H, Gater R, Goldberg D. (1998). *Randomized trial of the impact of school health program in rural Rawalpindi*, Pakistan, Lancet 352:1022-1025.

Raguram, R., Weiss, M.G., Channabasavanna, S.M., & Devins, G. M. (1996).Stigma, depression and somatization in South Africa. *AM. J. Psychiatry* 153, 1043-1049

Read, U.M., Adibokan, E. & Nyame, S. (2009). Local suffering and global discourse of mental illness in rural Ghana. *Global Health*, 5:13

Riedel-Pfaefflin, U. & Smith, A. (2010). Notes on diversity and working together across cultures on traumatization and forgiveness: sibling by choice: *Springer Science and Business Media*, 59(457-469).

Ritsher J.B. & Phelan J.C. (2004). Internalized stigma predicts erosion of morale among psychiatric out patients. *Psychiatric Research*, 129, 257-265

Roberts, H. (2001). A way forward for mental health care in Ghana? *The Lancet*, vol. 357

Rudell, K., Bhui, K, & Priebe, S. (2009). Concept, development and application of a new mixed method assessment of cultural variations in illness perceptions: Barts Explanatory Model Inventory: *Journal of Health Psychology*, 14, 336-347

Rutz, W. (2001). Mental health in Europe: problems, advances and challenges. *Acta psychiatry scand supplementary*, 410: 15-20

Samuel, O. A; Olusegun, M; Temilola & Funmilayo, F; Adejuwon. (2018). Rehabilitation of drug abusers: *The role of perceptions, relationships and family support, Social Work in Public Health*, 33:5, 289-298

Senreich, E. & Olusesi, O. A. (2016). Attitudes of West African immigrants in the United States towards substance misuse: Exploring culturally informed prevention and treatment strategies. *Social Work in Public Health*, vol. 31, (3), 153-167.

Shannon, P.J., Wieling, E., Simmelink-Mccleary, J. & Becher, E. (2015). Beyond stigma: Barriers to discussing mental health in refugee population. *Journal of Loss and Trauma*, 20: 281-296

Sodi T. (2009). Indigenous healers diagnostic and treatment methods for illness and dysfunctions. Indilinga: *African Journal of Indigenous Knowledge System*, 8, 60-73

Stefanovics, E. A., He, H., Cavalcanti, M., Neto, H., Ofori-Atta, A., Leddy, M., Ighodaro, A., & Rosenheck, R. (2016). Witchcraft and Bi- psychosocial Causes of Mental Illness: Attitudes and Belief about mental illness among health professionals in five countries. *Journal of nervous and mental disease* (204), 3

Summerton J. V. (2006). The organization and infrastructure of the African traditional healing system: Reflection from a sub-district of South Africa. *African Studies*, 65, 297-319

Tanner R.E. (1999). Concerns, cooperation, and coexistence in healing. *British Medical Journal*, 319, 133

Tawiah, P.E., Adongo, P.B., Aikins, M. (2015). Mental health related stigma and discrimination in Ghana: Experience of patients and their caregivers, *Ghana Medical Journal*, vol. 49, 1

Thome E.S, Dargel A.A, Mighavacca, F.M. et al., (2013). Stigma experiences in bipolar patients: The impact upon functioning: *Journal of Psychiatric and Mental and Health Nursing*, 19, 665-671

Tilahun, D., Hanlon, C., Araya, M., Davey, B., Hoekstra, R.A. & Fekadu, A. (2007). Training needs and perspectives of community health workers in relation to integrating child mental health care into primary health care in a rural settings in Sub-Sahara Africa: a mixed methods study. *International Journal of Mental Health Systems*, 11:15

U.S. Department of Health and Human Services (1979). The Belmont Report: Ethical Principles and Guidelines for the Protection of Human Subjects of Research. Retrieved from http://www. hhs.gov/ohrp/humansubjects/guidance/belmont.htm#xbenefit on May 28, 2019.

Van Beck, A. M. (2010). A cross-cultural case for convergence in pastoral thinking and training; *the multicultural proficiency project,* 59 (471-481)

Walker, G. H. (2015). Ghana Mental Health Act 846 2012: *A Qualitative Study of the Challenges and Priorities for Implementation. Ghana Medical Journal,* Vol. 49(4)

Waterman, S; Hunter, E. C; Cole, C.L; Evans, L.J; Greenburg, N; Rubin, G.J. & Beck, A. (2018). Training peers to treat Ebola center workers with anxiety and depression in Sierra Leon, *International Journal of Social Psychiatry,* Vol. 64(2) 156-165

Watson, A.C., Corrigan, P., Larson, J.E., Sells, M. (2007). Self-stigma in people with mental illness: *Schizophrenia Bull,* 33(6): 1312-1318

World Health Organization (2012).Fourth meeting of the WHO mental Health Gap Action Program (mhGAP) Forum. (cited February 9, 2019). Available from: URL: http://www.who.int/ mental_health/mhgap

Yang, C. P. & Lu, F.G. (2007). Indigenous and cultural psychology: understanding people in context; *Transpersonal Psychology Perspective,* 56 (105-113)

Yendork, J. et al., (2018). Mental illness has multiple causes: beliefs on causes of mental illness by congregants of selected neo-prophetic churches in Ghana. *Mental Health, Religion & Culture,* p. 647-666

Yendork, J. S; Kpobi, L. & Sarfo, E. A. (2016). "It is only madness that I know": *Analysis of how mental is conceptualized by congregants of selected charismatic churches in Ghana. Mental Health, Religion and Culture,* Vol. 19(9), 984-99

United Nations African News, Retrieved on June, 1st 2019 from: www.un.org/africarenewal/magazine/mental-illness-invisible-devastating.

CHAPTER EIGHT

APPENDICES

Explanation of Some Key Terms Utilized in the Study (Sort of - Glossary of Terms):

Snow Ball Recruitment Method

The snowball recruitment method also referred to as snowball sampling or chain referral, is used to recruit participants for a study by allowing participants to hire people they know are capable of being in the study, as we noted it in our abstract and body of work. The participants use their contacts to add more potential people to the study, especially, when getting right participants for an investigation is not easy to be found, or the population under study is hidden to reach potential participants for the study (Bowne, 2007).

Mental Illness Stigmatization Scale (MISS)

It is a method to address mental illness stigma through an understanding of stigma processes, the cause, and factors that may lead a person from shame to its negative consequences. It involves using critical questions to understand, observe, and measure stigma in the area of stereotyping, discrimination, separation, and labeling (Link et al., 2004).

Likert Scale

Likert scale is used to rate study questions ranging from one extreme (strongly agree) to another height (strongly disagree). Basically, Likert Scale is a scaling system where respondents are asked to rate items on a level of agreement or disagreement, like strongly agree, simply agrees, or slightly disagrees etc). The level uses 5 to 7 items to understand people's perception of questions, and it includes mid-point questions for people who are neutral on the issue to answer. The Likert scale also helps to detect respondent's feelings and attitude about a study as to know those that firmly believe and those with a superficial perspective on the research questions

Belmont Report

The National Commission created the Belmont report for the protection of human subjects of Biomedical and Behavioral Research. The essence of the principle is to have a guideline that will ensure researches that involved in human subjects follow the basic principle of beneficence, justice, and respect for persons utilized in the study. The Belmont principle assists in resolving ethical problems surrounding the conduct of research with human subjects (United States Department of Health, 1979). The Belmont principle task was to consider the boundaries between Biomedical and Behavioral research, the risk-benefit of the human subject, the selection of research participants, and the informed consent in the study.

Beneficence Principle

It is an act of kindness or charity used in the Belmont Report to express action in the "do not harm" to maximize benefits and minimize harm with regards to conducting research (United States Department of Health, 1979). The Beneficence Principle calls on professionals to favor the well-being and interest of their clients (Kinsinger, 2009).

Ethnography:

The word ethnography originated from anthropology and sociology. It is a research method to study the shared patterns of behavior, language, and action of a cultural group for some time. Ethnography covers the culture, sub-culture, or program in the society, and allows the learning of the culture of the people. Ethnography helps to understand the culture of certain parts of the world positively or negatively. It assists in analyzing people and their culture through interviews, observation, and documentation.

Thematic Analysis:

It is used in qualitative research to examine, pinpoint, and document patterns or themes within interview data. The essence is to gain knowledge from interview data and utilize it to validate ideas from the research.

Lightning Source UK Ltd.
Milton Keynes UK
UKHW010638090820
367887UK00001B/17/J